# Exegetical Preaching

Spiros Zodhiates, Th.D.

## 52 Exegetical Outlines
## Volume 1

# Exegetical Preaching

Spiros Zodhiates, Th.D.

# 52 Exegetical Outlines
# Volume 1

AMG
PUBLISHERS
Chattanooga, Tennessee

**Exegetical Preaching**
**Volume One**

Softcover edition, 1998

ISBN 0–89957–485–8

*Printed in the United States of America*
03 02 01 00 99 98 –R– 6 5 4 3 2 1

*To*
*Dr. and Mrs. Donald Schlernitzauer,*
*my beloved ophthamologist and his wife, who graciously spent much time*
*in editing many of these outlines originally written for "Pulpit and Bible*
*Study Helps"*

# CONTENTS

Preface                                                              vii

1. How Does the Christian Influence
   This World?                          Matt. 5:13–16              1

2. Putting Christ First                 Matt. 16:21–28             3

3. When a Brother Sins against You      Matt. 18:15–20            7

4. Changing Your Mind Can Be
   Blessed or Disastrous                Matt. 21:28–32           10

5. Jesus and the Sabbath                Mark 2:23—3:6            14

6. Salvation Is Like Vegetation         Mark 4:26–34             17

7. No Cross, No Power                    Mark 8:31–38             19

8. Did Jesus Permit Divorce?            Mark 10:2–16             22

9. The Transfiguration of Jesus Christ  Luke 9:28–36             26

10. Supremacy or Service                Luke 10:17–20            29

11. Luxury and Poverty                  Luke 16:19–31            33

12. The Trinity and the New Birth       John 3:1–17              37

13. Loving Is Obeying                    John 15:9–17             40

14. The Coming of the Holy Spirit       John 15:26, 27           43

15. The Meaning of Pentecost            Acts 2:1–21              46

16. Water Baptism and the Holy Spirit   Acts 8:14–23             51

17. God's Spirit in Control of Our Lives Rom. 8:14–17            53

18. No One Can Separate Us from
    God's Love                          Rom. 8:31–39             56

19. The Mystery of Christmas            Rom. 16:25–27            59

20. Warnings to Modern Day
    "Corinthians"                       1 Cor. 10:1–13           62

21. Victory over Temptation             1 Cor. 10:13             64

22. Confirmed Hope                      1 Cor. 15:19–26          68

23. Christ Makes Us New Creatures       2 Cor. 5:16–21           70

24. How to Live Victoriously in an
    Evil World                          Gal. 1:1–5               72

25. The True Gospel and Another Gospel  Gal. 1:1–10              77

Contents

26. The Ineffectiveness of the Law to
    Save or Sanctify                        Gal. 2:15–21        79
27. What Was the Function of the Law?       Gal. 3:23–29        81
28. How to Walk as Children of Light        Eph. 5:8–13         83
29. Free to Think as You Should             Phil. 2:5–11        89
30. The Ultimate in Expectations            Phil. 3:8–14        91
31. Guidelines for the Christian Life       Phil. 4:1–9         93
32. Do You Have Resurrection Life?          Col. 3:1–11         97
33. How Should a Christian Behave?          Col. 3:12–17        99
34. Why Should We Be Thankful?              1 Thess. 1:1–3     101
35. Paul's Model of an Effective Ministry   1 Thess. 2:1–8     105
36. What Kind of Joy Do You Want?           1 Thess. 5:16      109
37. How to Face Tribulation                 2 Thess. 1:3–10    113
38. God's Righteous Judgment on the
    Enemies of the Gospel                   2 Thess. 1:5–12    118
39. God Does Not Choose Without
    Sanctifying                             2 Thess. 2:13–15   120
40. Why Jesus Christ Came into
    the World                               1 Tim. 1:15        122
41. God Desires All People to Be Saved      1 Tim. 2:1–7       129
42. Godliness and Money                     1 Tim. 6:3–10      131
43. Feel Rich with What You Have            1 Tim. 6:3–19      137
44. Death Should Not Frighten Us            2 Tim. 2:8–15      139
45. What Is the Crown of Righteousness?     2 Tim. 4:6–8       141
46. Paul Did Not Practice Selfishness       Phile. 1:1–12      144
47. Our Glorification Through Suffering      Heb. 2:10–18       146
48. How to Fight in Order to Win            Heb. 12:1          151
49. The Temporal and the Eternal            Heb. 12:26         155
50. The Judgment of God                     1 Pet. 1:17–23     159
51. A Christian View of Suffering           1 Pet. 2:18, 19    162
52. The Beginning and the End               Rev. 1:8           165

    Index of Greek Words                                       169
    Scripture Index                                            292

# PREFACE

This book is a compilation of selected outlines which previously have been published in *Pulpit and Bible Study Helps,* a publication used by over 200,000 pastors and teachers of the Bible. These outlines are written to meet the need of those who follow the Lectionary, a system used by a number of churches. Each outline follows in order from Matthew to Revelation, one for every week of the year.

The unique features of this book include a key verse given for each outline, which is the focus of the entire passage the outline covers. In addition, an Index of Greek Words is provided listing each Greek word (transliterated) mentioned in the outlines along with a definition, the Scripture references where the word is found (if applicable), and the page number where each word occurs.

My prayer is that this volume of outlines will serve to be beneficial to those of you who are involved in teaching and preaching God's Word.

Spiros Zodhiates

# How Does the Christian Influence This World?

Key Verse: Matthew 5:16

---

I. **The World Can Be Divided into Two Kinds of People**
   A. First, there are the believers who in the Beatitudes are called blessed (*makárioi*), indwelt by God because of Christ (Matt. 5:3–12). They are the people who realize their spiritual helplessness, show sorrow over sin, and who are meek (or balanced between extremes), hungry for God's righteousness, merciful, pure in heart, peace-makers, ridiculed, persecuted, or slandered because of Christ. Jesus compares them to salt and light.
   B. The other group consists of the unbelievers of this world. They are proud, self-sufficient, and do not understand their own unrighteousness before a Holy God.

II. **The Believer Influences the Unbeliever by What He Is, Not by What He Has**
   A. Christ did not say, "You have salt and light to dispense," but rather "Ye are the salt. . . . Ye are the light of the world" (Matt. 5:13, 14). The believer's very presence in the world acts as salt and light, preventing corruption and exposing error.
   B. Being blessed means having God's nature within (2 Pet. 1:4). Because of Christ, the believers are no longer "fornicators, nor idolaters, nor adulterers, nor effeminate, nor abusers of themselves with mankind, nor thieves, nor covetous, nor drunkards, nor revilers, nor extortioners" (1 Cor. 6:9, 10). Rather, they "are

washed . . . sanctified . . . justified in the name of the Lord Jesus, and by the Spirit of our God" (1 Cor. 6:11). Indeed, they are "a peculiar people" (Titus 2:14) who are observed by unbelievers. The word translated "peculiar" is perioúsios which means "who constitute His possession." It is the difference in their character which distinguishes them.

C. The adjective *makários* (blessed) means not only indwelt by God because of Christ, but also being fully satisfied. Having obtained peace with God through Christ, the believer is more fulfilled than if he had all the world as his possession (Matt. 16:26; Mark 8:36; Luke 9:25). Seeing the believers' contentment despite poverty and physical suffering, the unbelievers are amazed (2 Cor. 6:10). It may even cause them to see their own lack of spiritual security in spite of worldly goods (Rev. 3:17).

## III. The Believer Must Interact with This World of Corruption and Darkness in Order to Act as Salt and Light

A. Just as salt is derived from the earth, so every believer is to remember that he is earthly, *epígeios* (2 Cor. 5:1). However, in Christ he becomes "free from the law of sin and death" (Rom. 8:2). Thereby, he acts as a preservative in the decaying world around him. Should he lose his Christ-likeness, "his savor" (Matt. 5:13), he would no longer be of any use.

B. Likewise, the believer is light because Christ is the "light of the world" (John 8:12). He can only reflect Christ's light. Therefore, Jesus admonishes him, "Let your light so shine before men, that they may see your good works, and glorify your Father which is in heaven" (Matt. 5:16). One day the total universe, *kósmos* (John 8:12), will be completely transformed by Christ. The believer's life should manifest the beginning of that transformation.

# Putting Christ First

Key Verse: Matthew 16:24

---

## I. True Disciples Are Devoted to Christ

A. There are three characteristics of man: self, family, possessions. Anyone who places these before the Lord Jesus, cannot be His disciple. This is clearly delineated in the words of Christ.

    1. "If any man will come after me, let him deny himself" (Matt. 16:24). Love for oneself is a standard for measuring the amount of love we have for others (Matt. 19:19; 22:39; Mark 12:31; Luke 10:27). Love for self is innate and is the primary concern of an unbeliever.

    2. "If any man come to me, and hate not his father, and mother, and wife, and children, and brethren, and sisters, yea, and his own life also, he cannot be my disciple" (Luke 14:26).

    3. "So likewise, whosoever he be of you that forsaketh not all that he hath, he cannot be my disciple" (Luke 14:33).

B. Christ did not conceal from inquirers who wanted to follow Him what the grace of God would accomplish in a believer. He did not promise eternal life which resides dormant in the human heart. He offered God's grace which brings a complete change by putting Christ's new life in man. The old nature which puts self, family, or possessions first, is put off by the new nature. "Lie not one to another, seeing that ye have put off the old man with his deeds" (Col. 3:9). This "putting off" of the old man is equivalent to believing on the Lord Jesus. It takes God's grace to do this (Eph. 2:8). Christ comes to dwell within us. Our old Adamic nature no longer has uncontested control, but it is not eliminated. Paul had this struggle between the victorious nature of Christ within him and the sin that still dwelt in him. This is why he said, "It is no more I that do it, but sin that dwelleth in me" (Rom. 7:17).

C. When an unbeliever understands what will automatically take place as a result of salvation, he may be honest enough to reject it like the rich young ruler who came to Jesus (Matt. 19:16–22; Mark 10:17–22; Luke 18:18–23). Jesus told him what must happen in his life for him to receive Christ's grace or eternal life: he must be willing to give up his possessions. Jesus knew that this was not what the man wanted to do but this did not change His declaration of truth. Therefore the man remained rich materially, but spiritually poor.

D. The Lord Jesus in no way demands that all who follow Him sell all their belongings and give them to the poor. However, when He saves a person, He must be first in that person's life. Family and possessions must be available for the altar of sacrifice for His sake. The same Christ who told this young man "sell that thou hast, and give to the poor" (Matt. 19:21) also said "But seek ye first the kingdom of God, and his righteousness; and all these things shall be added unto you" (Matt. 6:33). This same Christ also said "For what is a man profited, if he shall gain the whole world, and lose his own soul? or what shall a man give in exchange for his soul?" (Matt. 16:26). What Christ impresses us with is that with Jesus Christ first in our hearts and lives we are always winners. When Jesus Christ is first, I fully enjoy myself, my family, and my possessions. All life is then subject to His command and direction.

## II. The Call to Cross-Bearing Was for All Who Would Follow Jesus

A. The fact that Jesus was speaking to His disciples in Matthew 16:21, 24 has given some people the wrong impression that the call to be a disciple of the Lord Jesus is only addressed to believers.

B. In Mark 8:34, however, we see that He was not speaking to his disciples only, "And when he had called the people unto him with his disciples also. . ." and also in Luke 9:23, "And he said to them all. . . ."

C. He did not address His disciples directly when He said "If any man will come after me" (Matt. 16:24); "Whosoever will come after me . . ." (Mark 8:34); "If any man will come after me . . ." (Luke 9:23). These apply to non-believers just as John 3:16 does. Jesus wanted those who would truly follow Him as His disciples to know that the acceptance of His grace revolutionizes an individual. Christ not only comes to live within, but there is a constant renewal of the new nature which gives the old self last place. There is a glory of grace that no love of self, relatives, or possessions can give. The call to be disciples is to all men, and the first step is trusting in Him for eternal life.

## III. A Disciple of Christ Lives a Balanced Life

A. The Greek verb in Luke 14:33 translated "forsaketh" explains the philosophy of a disciple of Christ. "So likewise, whosoever he be of you that forsaketh not all that he hath, he cannot be my disciple." The Greek word is *apotássomai* derived from *apó*, "from, or away from oneself," and *tássomai* which means "to place in the proper category." The Lord never taught reckless abandonment of self, relatives, or possessions. He wants us as believers to put them where they belong. They should come after Christ. We should never love God with the love which belongs to self, family, and possessions. The love we have for Him should be unique, leading us to worship. When we give Him the proper love, then our love for others and temporary possessions will fall into its proper place.

B. Jesus Christ asserts that a true believer is a disciple who, by constant learning and devotion, loses himself for the sake of his glorious Savior (Matt. 16:24–28; Mark 8:34—9:1; Luke 9:23–27). The joy of the believer, however, is proportionate to his obedience to Christ.

# When a Brother Sins Against You

Key Verse: Matthew 18:15

---

I. Remember That You Are Not Sinless and You Cannot Expect Others to Be

A. The word "if" in Matthew 18:15 is the Greek *eán* which is a suppositional conjunction of objective possibility. It is a situation likely to occur, not a subjective supposition which may never be realized (usually indicated by the Greek particle *ei*). Don't live in a dream world thinking that your brother in Christ is so perfect that he will never do anything to offend you.

B. The verb "trespass" in Matthew 18:15 is in the subjunctive aorist (*hamartḗsē*) which indicates not a life of sin, but a single act. It basically means to miss the mark. You set the mark for your brother but somehow he misses it. He does not measure up to your expectations. This happens so easily. We meet our own aim, but often miss the goals others set for us.

II. No Indifference Is Allowed in the Life of the Christian Toward Another

A. This does not mean, however, that we have the right to pry into the lives of others in order to find a reason to correct them. Our Lord gave us clear command not to judge others in Matthew 7:1, 2, "Judge not, that ye be not judged. For with what judgment ye judge, ye shall be judged: and with what measure ye mete, it shall be measured to you again." No one has the right to be a self-appointed judge of others. The commandment, "Judge not," is in the present indicative entailing continuity of action.

B. Christ teaches in Matthew 18:15 that if you are offended because your brother fails to meet your standard in something particular, you should go to him. This only involves something personal as indicated by the phrase "against thee." It does not say that you should take up the cause if it is against someone else. It must be something which affects you and you alone.

C. Your brother may be totally unconscious of the thing he has done to disappoint you. If you refuse to see him about it, you may continue to harbor feelings against him, which would be harmful to you.

## III. The Injured Person Must Go to the One Who Offended

A. Let it be a private matter. Instead of telling others, go and reprove him. The verb *élegxon* is the aorist imperative active of *elégchō*, "to rebuke, reprove." This indicates a once and for all action. It implies that the brother is in the wrong for whatever he did against his brother.

B. The purpose of going to him is to win him. If you do not make him aware of the problem, he will continue sinning to his own detriment. The approach of the injured is redemptive ". . . if he shall hear thee, thou hast gained thy brother."

C. The meaning of the verb "hear" (*akouō*) is "to heed or obey" which proves that the injurious person needs to amend his way.

## IV. Continuing to Harm a Brother Is Inadmissible in a Church Body

A. If the offending person does not heed the reproof of the injured person, he must be given a second opportunity to "shape up" in the presence of other witnesses (Matt. 18:16).

B. If this reproof is also rejected it should be brought before the church or the governing body of the church (Matt. 18:17).

C. The church is then given authority to deal with such a person as if he were a heathen, and no more a brother. Others must know that he is no longer part of the church and that he has been properly disciplined.

# Changing Your Mind Can Be Blessed or Disastrous

Key Verse: Matthew 21:29

---

I. The Context of the Parable of the Two Sons
   A. The parable comes in response to the question the chief priests and elders asked Jesus as He taught in the temple, ". . . By what authority doest thou these things? and who gave thee this authority?" (Matt. 21:23).
      1. Jesus refused to answer their question directly since they declined to answer His own question concerning the source of John the Baptist's baptism.
      2. Yet this parable provides an indirect answer, as is shown by the connective "but" which begins it.
   B. This parable is presented as a vivid pictorial challenge to the Jewish leaders.
      1. In Matthew 3:4–6 we find a first group responding to the message of repentance by John. But they came to John after their change of mind and regret for their sinful way of life. They feared that the Messiah would have nothing to do with them. The first son is representative of this group.
      2. In Matthew 3:7–10 are the religious characters which parallel the second son in the parable who said he would obey and yet, in the end, did not.
      3. The specific explanation and application is found in Matthew 21:31, 32. These religious leaders saw only too well that Jesus was referring to them (Matt. 21:45, 46).

## II. The Content of the Parable

A. A father had two children growing up.

1. The word used in this parable is *tékna*, "children," not *huioí*, "sons," who are old enough to decide what they are going to do in life, which word is used in the parable for the prodigal son in Luke 15:11–32.

2. In this parable we have two children who had not yet carved their careers nor made any final choices.

B. The father invited both sons to go and work in his vineyard. The duty of every father is to instill in his children the necessity and blessing of work.

1. The children must recognize the field is still their father's although they are called to work in it. "Son, go work today in my vineyard" (Matt. 21:28).

2. As laborers, children at work, we must never lose sight of the fact that it is not our world, it is His. "The field is the world" as Jesus said (Matt. 13:38). The whole world is His vineyard for His children to work in.

C. These two children were of the same father and yet they were so different.

1. When the second son is introduced, the Greek text in some manuscripts is *tō hetérō* which means "the other who was of different makeup and outlook."

2. The first child said, "I don't want to go" (Matt. 21:29).

   *a)* He voiced the instant inclination of his sinful nature. Tell a child to do something or go somewhere and the likely answer will be "I don't want to" (*ou thélō*) or as the KJV has it "I will not" (Matt. 21:29).

   *b)* "Afterward he repented and went." How much afterward? In Greek the adverb is *hústeron* which implies not immediately afterwards, but toward

11

the end of the thought process. It has more the
meaning of "finally."

3. The other child is differently disposed but the challenge of the father was the same. Work is for all.
This child said "I'll go," but he did not.

## III. The Change of Mind Which Means Repentance

A. The word most commonly translated "repentance" in
the New Testament is *metonoéō*, derived from *metá*,
"after," and *noéō*, "to think, perceive."

1. It means to change one's mind, which involves an
instantaneous change of heart, a regret for unbelief
and sin, and a determination to change direction.

2. This is what both John the Baptist (Matt. 3:2) and
the Lord Jesus preached: "Repent: for the kingdom
of God is at hand" (Matt. 4:17). Real repentance
(*metánoia*) results in the forgiveness or removal of
sin (Mark 1:4; Luke 3:3; Acts 2:38).

B. This is not the word used in Matthew 21:29: ". . . but
afterward he repented and went."

1. The Greek verb here is not *metánoēsas*, but *meta-
melētheís*, the passive participle of *metamélomai*,
derived from *metá*, "after," and *mélomai*, "to care or
show concern for oneself."

2. It means to regret, not because one feels he has
done anything wrong but because something did
not turn out to his own advantage. A thief when
caught regrets stealing not because he has con-
cluded that stealing is a sin, but because he was
caught. Such a person, however, has not become
moral if he does not steal anymore.

3. *Metánoia* represents moral change in an individual
while *metaméleia* is a convenient, selfish change of
behavior and regret.

*a)* This verb *metamélomai* is the verb used of Judas in Matthew 27:3, "Then Judas, which had betrayed him, when he saw that he [Jesus] was condemned, repented himself [*metameléthe*í*s*] and brought again the thirty pieces of silver to the chief priests and elders."

*b)* This was mere regret and not true repentance. Judas was not saved at the end, but he proved himself to be what he always was, the son of perdition (John 17:12). It is this verb *metamélomai* that is used in Matthew 21:29, 32.

## IV. The Application of This Parable
A. A prophetic application
1. The first son or child represents the Gentiles who were expected to say "no" at the beginning but in the end said "yes," and are now ahead of the unbelieving Jews (Rom. 10:18b–21).
2. The second son is representative of the Jewish nation. Jesus was of their own nationality. "Yes" was the immediate response expected, but then they changed their mind about Jesus and this change became disastrous (Rom. 9:1–10, 18).
3. God is not yet through with the second son who will change his mind again and say "yes" (Rom. 11).
B. A personal application
1. Your initial response to Christ may be a "no." Change your mind and be blessed.
2. Was your initial response a hurried "yes" without sufficient thought? Have you found that no fruit has come from your flippant "yes"? Change your mind by allowing the gospel to take root and bring forth fruit.

# Jesus and the Sabbath

Key Verse: Mark 2:27

---

I. **God Instituted the Sabbath as a Day of Rest**
   A. "Sabbath" means a desisting or cessation with more of a negative than a positive connotation. It is a day in which one should not do what he ordinarily does the other six days of the week (Ex. 23:12). God had a humanitarian motive for instituting this injunction against work on the Sabbath.
   B. The same benevolent purpose also lay behind the sabbatical year which was to be observed every seventh year (Ex. 23:11).
   C. In the Decalogue (Ex. 20:8) the Israelites were commanded to "Remember the sabbath day, to keep it holy [to set it apart from the others]," with further explanation of the command given in verses nine and ten. Deuteronomy 5:14 reveals the Lord's philanthropic intent that rest should also be given to others.
   D. Besides being a day of refreshment, the Sabbath was likewise a day of corporate worship, commemorating God's goodness (Ex. 20:11; Deut. 5:15).
   E. As time went on, however, the Sabbath celebration degenerated into mere legalistic prohibitions which sapped from it God's original altruistic intent. Our Lord explicitly refuted the rigid restrictions which had developed by saying, "The sabbath was made for man, and not man for the sabbath" (Mark 2:27). It was not to be seen as an end in itself but as a means to an end. The Sabbath was, therefore, instituted to bless man and bring honor to God.

## II. Why Did Jesus Choose the Sabbath Day to Show His Benevolence?

A. The Lord deliberately performed many of His miracles on the Sabbath.

1. One such miracle was the healing of the infirm man near the Pool of Bethesda (John 5:5–18). According to tradition it was lawful to carry a sick person on a bed on the Sabbath because the bed was only an accessory, but to carry the bed alone, an ordinary burden, was unlawful. Thus the healed man was criticized for carrying his bed, and Jesus was censored for healing on the Sabbath a man who was not dying (Mark 3:1–6).

2. The casting out of an unclean spirit at Capernaum also occurred on the Sabbath (Mark 1:21–27; Luke 4:33–37).

3. Jesus cured Peter's mother-in-law on the Sabbath after He had returned from the synagogue (Matt. 8:14, 15; Mark 1:29–31; Luke 4:38, 39).

4. Jesus also healed the man with a withered hand in the synagogue during Sabbath observances (Matt. 12:9–14; Mark 3:1–6; Luke 6:6–11).

5. Both the opening of the eyes of one born blind and the "making of clay" which was involved in this healing, brought criticism upon Jesus because they had been done on the Sabbath (John 9:1–16).

6. Jesus healed the woman who had a spirit of infirmity on the Sabbath (Luke 13:10–17).

7. He cured the man with the dropsy at the home of one of the chief Pharisees on the Sabbath as well (Luke 14:1–6).

B. By enacting all these miracles on the Sabbath, Jesus endeavored to show the true benevolent spirit of the Law. At the very beginning of His ministry He had declared, "Think not that I am come to destroy the law, or the prophets: I am not come to destroy, but to fulfill" (Matt. 5:17). Jesus thus attempted to restore to the Sabbath its original intent as He also did with other commandments (Matt. 15:3–20; 23:13–33).

C. By allowing His disciples to pluck corn on the Sabbath (Mark 2:23–28), Jesus showed that physical needs are to be met on the Sabbath as well. His illustration from the life of David (Matt. 12:3, 4; Mark 2:25, 26) likewise demonstrated that physical needs take precedence over the ceremonial law. Jesus explained that God prefers mercy exercised by man toward his fellows, to sacrifices (Matt. 12:7).

## III. After Christ's Resurrection, the Day of Worship Began to Be Observed on the First Day of the Week

A. During His earthly life and ministry the Lord Jesus honored the seventh day as a day of worship and took care to demonstrate its original beneficent purpose.

B. The first day of the week was instituted by the disciples of Christ not as a substitution for the Jewish Sabbath, but as a way of commemorating the Lord's resurrection (Acts 20:7; 1 Cor. 16:2). Although Jesus could have risen on the Sabbath, He rose instead in the early morning hours of the first day. In Greek that first day came to be called *kuriakē* (from *kúrios*, "Lord"), the day of the Lord (Rev. 1:10).

C. During the first three Christian centuries the Lord's Day was carefully distinguished from the Sabbath. It was only after the third century that these Christian and Jewish institutions gradually became confused.

# Salvation Is Like Vegetation

Key Verse: Mark 4:26

---

I. **In the Parable of the Growing Seed (found only in Mark 4:26–29), Jesus Compared Salvation to Vegetation**
   A. Just as God created the world without man's assistance, He also established the kingdom of God in the hearts of His people (Luke 17:20, 21) through the coming of His Son, Jesus Christ (Matt. 3:2).
   B. God has chosen, however, to appoint men as His coworkers in both the physical and spiritual realms. In agriculture the farmer sows the seed and then waits for growth to occur.
   C. Likewise, in the spiritual sphere, we are to speak and demonstrate the Word of God (Luke 8:11) to those around us. Then we must wait for God to work in their lives (1 Cor. 3:6, 7).
   D. Just as the power of life and growth is in the seed, so also is it in the Word of God. Man only assists in the process by disseminating God's truth abroad, just as a farmer casts the seed.

II. **After Sowing the Seed, the Man in the Parable Left the Matter in God's Hands**
   A. Instead of staying up all night worrying about it, he went about his business as usual (v. 27). In spiritual matters we should not fret either but allow the Holy Spirit to do His work.
   B. During this time "the seed springs up and grows up and he does not know how it takes place." The man could observe but not explain what God accomplished in the growth of the seed.

1. The Greek verb translated "spring" is *blastáne*, germinate, from the noun *blastós*, which means "germ." A man-made seed will never germinate. However, "The Word of God is quick [*zón*, 'living'], and powerful [*energés*, 'energizing'] . . ." (Heb. 4:12) as opposed to man's wisdom, which never will give rise to spiritual life.

2. "Grow up" in Greek is *mekúnetai*, which means "lengthen." Again, this action is of God, not man. The farmer is careful not to disturb the growth of a tender young shoot. Likewise, we should not try to hasten maturity in a young believer. He is equally fragile.

C. The stages in the growth of the plant have been determined by God and occur automatically: "First the blade, then the ear, after that the full corn in the ear" (Mark 4:28). Spiritual growth also follows a preordained pattern which we cannot change.

## III. Finally, the Farmer Harvested the Fruit

A. After planting the seed and waiting patiently for God to make it mature into fruit, the farmer then harvested it at the opportune moment (v. 29).

B. Again, God calls us into action at the proper time. The faith which He has produced in a believer needs to be channeled in appropriate ways to benefit the body of Christ and contribute to its growth. Edifying each other in this manner (Eph. 4:16), we may be likened to the farmer who reaps the harvest and then makes it into nourishment for himself and others.

# No Cross, No Power

Key Verse: Mark 8:35

---

I. **Jesus Could Have Avoided the Cross but He Did Not**
   A. He had the power to avoid it.
      1. He explicitly stated so in John 10:18: "No man taketh it [my life] from me, but I lay it down of myself. I have power to lay it down, and I have power to take it again. . . ."
      2. If you had this kind of power would you ever voluntarily die?
   B. If He had avoided it, He would not have realized the very purpose of His incarnation.
      1. "The Word . . . was made flesh" (John 1:14). Why? Because blood is in the flesh and without the shedding of blood there can be no remission of sin (Heb. 9:22).
      2. People do not come into the world merely to live, for that is no better than being an animal. We also have "spirit" in addition to a soul and body. To fail to accomplish the purpose for which God destined us, is to miss the real joy of life.
      3. Can you imagine Christianity without the cross and the consequent resurrection? It would be only one of many religions. It would not be the transforming "power of God unto salvation" (Rom. 1:16).

II. **Jesus Spoke about the Necessity of the Cross**
   A. The little word "must" in Matthew 16:21, Mark 8:31, and Luke 9:22 is arresting. In Greek it is the impersonal *dei* which means "it is necessary."

B. He did not die because the situation was unavoidable.

C. It was necessary that He die because this was how He would redeem us and bring us into fellowship with God. It was the "must" of duty.

## III. He Made His Announcement Only after Peter's Great Confession about His Being the Christ

A. He was recognized as the divinely anointed of God.

B. As a mere man He would not have died while He had the power to live.

C. As people indwelt by God and participants in the divine nature (2 Pet. 1:4), we choose duty before life, the cross before pleasure and enjoyment of this world. If we are not characterized by this divine nature, we are none of His. This is clearly stated in Mark 8:34, "Whosoever will come after me, let him deny himself, and take up his cross, and follow me."

D. Those who believe that they can bypass the cross are not truly Christ's. Jesus called Peter "Satan" because he rebuked Jesus for not escaping death although He possessed the power to do so (Matt. 16:22, 23).

## IV. There Were No Short-Cuts to Success

A. The first one to suggest success and achievement without the cross was Satan himself.

B. Jesus objected to the miracles Satan wanted Him to perform. Satan suggested that Jesus should change useless stones into useful loaves of bread (Matt. 4:3).

C. We should watch out for those who have followed Satan's suggestion to perform "miracles" and have not "taken up their crosses" to follow Jesus. Beware of the preachers of the gospel of wealth and prosperity.

D. Satan wanted Jesus to acquire instant fame and he quoted Scripture to persuade Him to do so. Satan suggested that God would perform a miracle if Jesus would only cast Himself from the pinnacle of the temple.

E. Success from Christ's point of view is living in voluntary obscurity and self-effacement like Christ when you could live otherwise.

## V. He Who Had the Will to Die on the Cross Had the Power to Rise from the Dead

A. No other person on earth has ever said what Jesus said and accomplished it: "The Son of man must suffer many things, and be rejected of the elders and of the chief priests, and scribes, and be killed, and after three days rise again" (Mark 8:31).

B. He knew that by God's appointment He was to die but He was absolutely sure that on the third day He would rise from the dead.

C. Would the world be better had He chosen to live on, escape death and not exercise His power to rise from the dead?

D. As in His case, so in everyone He indwells: ". . . to live is Christ, and to die is gain" (Phil. 1:21).

# Did Jesus Permit Divorce?

Key Verse: Mark 10:9

---

I. God Intended Marriage to Be Permanent, but He Did Make Provision for Those Whose Spouses Are Unfaithful

    A. In the Old Testament God instituted marriage to be one man and one woman joined together for life (Gen. 2:24).

    B. Malachi 2:16 states that God "hateth putting away."

    C. In Deuteronomy 24:1–4, however, God gave a procedure for divorce because of the hardness of men's hearts (Mark 10:5).

        1. When a man put away his wife, he had to "write her a bill of divorcement."

        2. The bill of divorcement was really a certificate of innocence because, had the woman been immoral, she would have been stoned under the Law (Lev. 20:10; Deut. 22:21). The fact that she "may go and be another man's wife" shows that the charge against her was a fabricated one and that she was in fact innocent of unfaithfulness.

    D. Jesus reiterated this view of marriage in the New Testament (Matt. 5:27–32; 19:2–12; Mark 10:2–12; Luke 16:18; Rom. 7:1–3; 1 Cor. 7).

II. Divorce Is Not the Same Today

    A. In biblical times when a husband or wife would dismiss (*apoluō*) his or her marital partner unjustifiably without giving that partner "a bill of divorcement," they wanted others to conclude that there must have been inconstancy on the part of the dismissed person. They were not concerned that this innocent partner would be considered an adulterer. The Mosaic Law, when applied, protected such an innocent party.

B. Today, on the other hand, a judge can declare a marriage dissolved for any reason; a wife or husband cannot dismiss a marital partner on his or her own. The court does not necessarily distinguish between the unfaithful and innocent party. Therefore, there is no "bill of divorcement" to protect the innocent and condone remarriage.

## III. Christ Condemned the Guilty but Not the Innocent Party

A. God is a just God who executes justice (Rom. 2:5; 1 John 1:9; Rev. 15:3; 16:5, 7; 19:2).

B. He does not condemn the victim of a crime.

C. In the case of marriage, one of the two partners may decide to leave the other. Such divorce is sin if the dismissed partner is innocent of infidelity. The one that dismisses his partner in this instance must suffer the consequences of his own sin (Deut. 24:4).

D. But is it even conceivable that Christ, the holy and righteous God incarnate, would equally condemn the guilty party and the innocent partner who has been divorced? Impossible!

## IV. Christ Allowed for Divorce in the Case of Infidelity

A. In the case of infidelity, Jesus gave the innocent party the privilege of divorcing the guilty partner. This is the only basis on which divorce is permitted: ". . . for the cause of fornication. . ." (Matt. 5:32).

B. The believer's body is the temple or the dwelling place of the Holy Spirit (1 Cor. 6:19) and a member of the body of Christ (1 Cor. 6:15). If the believer is joined to a harlot (*pórnē*), he defiles not only his own body, but also the whole body of Christ. If an innocent wife continues to be joined together with a husband who engages in extramarital sex, then she contributes to the defilement of not only her own body, but likewise the body of Christ. The wife has to make the choice of either remaining married, with the hope that the fornicator will repent of his sin, or divorcing him (in which case she does not sin).

## V. A Study of the Greek Verbs Shows the Distinction Jesus Made Between the Innocent and Guilty

A. The verb meaning "to commit adultery" in Greek is *moicheúō*. It is used in the active voice in Matthew 5:27, 28; 19:18; Mark 10:19; Luke 16:18.

B. The phrase "to commit adultery" might also be expressed in Greek by the verb *moicháō*. This verb occurs in the New Testament only in the middle form *moichōmai*. It can be in the active, middle, or passive voice: commit adultery, commit adultery against oneself, have adultery committed against oneself, respectively.

1. In Matthew 5:32, "But, I say unto you, That whosoever shall put away his wife, saving for the cause of fornication [passive voice], causeth her to commit adultery [*moichásthai*, causes adultery upon her]: and whosoever shall marry her that is divorced committeth adultery." The verb here for "committeth adultery" is *moichátai*, the middle voice, which means he "causes adultery to come upon himself."

2. Matthew 19:9 is correctly translated, "Whosoever shall put away his wife, except it be for fornication, and shall marry another, committeth adultery [*moichátai* the middle voice, meaning 'commit

adultery against himself']: and whoso marrieth her which is put away doth commit adultery [*moichá-tai*, the middle voice meaning 'causes adultery upon himself']."

3. Mark 10:11, 12 states, "Whosoever shall put away his wife, and marry another, committeth adultery against her [*moichátai*, active meaning]. And if a woman shall put away her husband, and be married to another, she committeth adultery [*moichá-tai*, deponent active meaning]."

4. Luke 16:18 says, "Whosoever putteth away his wife, and marrieth another, committeth adultery [*moicheúei*, the active verb]: and whosoever marrieth her that is put away from *her* husband committeth adultery [*moicheúei*, the active verb]." The expression "her that is put away from her husband" may be mistaken as the innocent, dismissed wife. In this instance, the Greek is "the one who dismissed herself from [her] husband," showing that she is the guilty one and her husband, the innocent one. Therefore, whosoever marries this woman, commits adultery. However, when one is innocent, he does not commit adultery if he remarries.

# The Transfiguration of Jesus Christ

Key Verse: Luke 9:29

---

I. **When and Where Did the Transfiguration Occur?**
   A. Luke 9:28 says, ". . . about an eight days after these sayings. . ." while Matthew 17:1 and Mark 9:2 read, "And after six days. . . ." There is no discrepancy in these accounts. Luke simply included the day of the Transfiguration and the day of "these sayings" while Matthew and Mark excluded them, counting only the six days in between the two events.
   B. The Transfiguration is believed to have occurred at Caesarea Philippi the location of the highest mountain in the area, Mt. Hermon, which rises to an elevation of 9,232 feet. It is specifically referred to as a "high mountain" in two of the accounts (Matt. 17:1; Mark 9:2).

II. **What Were the Events and Sayings Which Preceded Jesus' Transfiguration?**
   A. First, in response to Jesus' question "But whom say ye that I am?" Peter made his great confession about Jesus being "the Christ, the Son of the living God" (Matt. 16:16); "the Christ" (Mark 8:29); "the Christ of God" (Luke 9:20). All of us must still answer this same question today.
   B. Next, Jesus had predicted His own death and resurrection (Matt. 16:21–27; Mark 8:31–37; Luke 9:21–26).
   C. Peter was shocked and objected to the idea of Jesus' death since He had the power to avoid it. Jesus then

rebuked Peter, calling him "Satan" (Matt. 16:23; Mark 8:33). Let us learn from Peter's mistake not to call Jesus "Christ" and then deny His sovereignty over the affairs of men.

III. **This Event Helped Explain the Last and Most Difficult Saying of Jesus in Matthew 16:28; Mark 9:1; and Luke 9:27**
   A. "There be some standing here, which shall not taste of death, till they see the Son of man coming in his kingdom." Jesus made this statement six days before the Transfiguration, which was a fulfillment of it. The three: Peter, James, and John were those who did "not taste of death" until they saw the glory of Jesus revealed just six days after Jesus made His prediction.
   B. This connection between the two events can be made because of the use of "and" connecting them in Matthew 17:1 and Mark 9:2, and the particle *de*, in Luke 9:28, translated "and."

IV. **The Transfiguration Foreshadowed the Second Coming of Christ**
   A. Scripture tells us that Christ will unexpectedly return (Matt. 24:44; Mark 13:32, 33; Luke 12:40, 46) and set up His kingdom just as He predicted (Matt. 16:28; Mark 9:1; Luke 9:27). The Transfiguration was a preview of this wondrous event to come.
   B. The transformation began with prayer between Christ and the Father (Luke 9:28). The infinitive used here is *proseúxasthai*, the aorist tense, which indicates a punctiliar action instead of the habitual practice of prayer. This event was going to be a special time of communion between the unique Son and His Father. What actually happened was that as Jesus prayed, He was "transfigured." In Mark 9:2 the Greek word is

*metemorphóthe*, derived from *metá*, "change of condition" and *morphóo*, "to form." The change which came upon the Man-God here was from the inside out. Luke says, "And as he prayed, the fashion of his countenance was altered, and his raiment was white and glistering." What is translated as "fashion" is *eídos*, meaning the external appearance of His face. It became different, *héteron*, qualitatively different, and His clothing, "white and glistering." White is the color of angelic garments (Mark 16:5; Acts 1:10; Rev. 3:4). The whole description of Christ then speaks of His heavenly kingship, which He will assume upon His Second Coming.

C. There also appeared two Old Testament personalities with Christ at His Transfiguration.

   1. The first was Moses, who represented those who have died in the Lord and will be raised to meet Christ in the air at His return (1 Thess. 4:16).

   2. The second person to appear was Elijah, who did not die but was taken into heaven alive (2 Kgs. 2:1). He represented those who will be alive at the coming of the Lord and who will be changed (1 Cor. 15:51, 52) as they also are taken up to be with Jesus (1 Thess. 4:17).

D. Therefore, the purpose of the Transfiguration was to give Peter, John, and James, as well as all believers to follow, a preview of the kingdom of God which we are to eagerly await.

# Supremacy or Service

Key Verse: Luke 10:20

---

I. **Man Longs for Supremacy instead of Service**
   A. It is unlikely that the messengers of Christ came back all at once.
      1. They had gone to every town and place that Jesus was going to visit (Luke 10:1).
      2. They probably came back in small groups; maybe "two by two" as they were sent (Luke 10:1).
      3. Not one couple apparently had a different report. The thing that impressed them most was how supremely they fared in the war against evil spiritual powers.
   B. Although they were handpicked by Jesus, these messengers demonstrated that they were not free from the passions of humanity.
      1. Many people love statistics that show how successful they have been in a mission for Christ.
      2. It is better to speak of service to humans than of conquest over devils.
      3. Beware of people who boast of their fights with Satan and their conquest over him.

II. **Our Main Task in Missions Is Not Fighting the Devil but Carrying Out the Lord's Will**
   A. Jesus had not given them any specific command to engage in a fight against evil spiritual forces.
      1. He told them that there was a harvest (Luke 10:2).
         *a*) He who sends us prepares the hearts to be reached.

*b*) We should never go forth fearing the possibility of failure.

*c*) There were seventy workers for a small area of Palestine where there were only a few villages.

*d*) The number of workers in proportion to the population was far greater than the proportion of preachers and missionaries to the populaton in our day, to our great shame.

2. They were to prepare the way for Him, but not to take His place (Luke 10:1).

3. They were sent with authority.

*a*) The verb Jesus used was *apostéllō*, "I send you." There was authority (*exousía*) attached to this command.

*b*) Jesus used the same verb in the sending of the Twelve (Matt. 10:5, 16, 40).

*c*) It was the same verb Jesus used to indicate His being sent by the Father (Luke 9:48; 10:16).

*d*) There was special authority granted to the Twelve and the seventy disciples to establish the authenticity of the gospel and of Jesus Christ.

*e*) When it came to the sending forth of all believers after His resurrection in John 20:21, Jesus used the word *pémpō*, which means "to send" not with authority, but "under authority." "As my Father hath sent me [*apéstalken*], even so send I [*pémpō*] you."

B. Indeed both the Twelve and the seventy disciples exercised these extraordinary powers, perhaps under the grand illusion that it was the greatest thing they could ever do.

1. The preaching of the gospel and its acceptance may have taken an inferior place in their ministry.

*a*) Observe what they declared about Jesus: "Lord, even the devils are subject unto us through thy name."

*b*) The word *kai* in Greek means "and," indicating that they did not fail to preach and heal (Luke 10:9). They had exhibited such power before, but to actually have evil powers obey them was a surprise.

*c*) Perhaps that is why the Lord gave such "authority" only to this small group of apostles and messengers.

2. Observe a correct translation of Mark 16:17, "And these signs shall follow them that believed [*tois pisteúsasi*, aorist participle]; in my name shall they cast out devils [*daimónia*, 'demons,' the same word used in Luke 10:17]; they shall speak with new tongues." This referred to what the apostles and the Twelve actually did.

C. It could be that they were puffed up.

1. They said, "Lord, even the devils are subject unto us" (Luke 10:17).

2. They thought they were very important! They thought they were special people with the authority to exorcise demons.

3. Of course they did acknowledge that Jesus had a part: "through thy name." Perhaps they felt that they were the performers and the influence of Jesus was minimal.

## III. Jesus Rebuked the Seventy Disciples

A. Jesus rebuked them not because what they did was wrong.

1. They preached the gospel.

2. They healed.

3. They exorcised demons.

B. He rebuked them because they emphasized the wrong things.

1. They were proud because they thought they had defeated the devil and his demons.

2. They thought that casting out devils was primary.

3. They forgot that their primary task was to preach and heal and then when the devil attacked (as he surely always does) he would not prevail.

4. The devil's activity is a reaction to God's children doing what God wants them to do for the souls and bodies of people. If we attempt to see the devil everywhere, then he will occupy all our time and keep us so busy fighting him that we will leave ourselves no time to preach the gospel. If he is able to engage us in constant battle, he will have succeeded in keeping us from the true fight that we as Christians should be fighting.

C. The most important thing that ever happened to the Twelve and the seventy disciples was that their names were written in the Book of Life in heaven. The most important task for any of Christ's messengers is to see that people's names are written in the Book of Life (Rev. 13:8; 17:8; 20:12; 21:27).

D. Knowing that people are saved from the eternal condemnation of sin should produce in us, as messengers of Christ, the greatest joy.

# Luxury and Poverty

## Key Verse: Luke 16:25

---

### I. Riches and Poverty Contrasted
  A. Riches
  1. Riches are a curse only if they hinder a person from entering God's kingdom (Matt. 19:23, 24; Luke 18:23) or draw him away from God.
  2. There were rich people who followed Jesus.
      *a*) Joseph of Arimathea (Matt. 27:57).
      *b*) Zacchaeus (Luke 19:2).
      *c*) The socially distinguished women ministered to Jesus out of their own resources (Luke 8:3).
  3. Riches can be a blessing if they are used properly and unselfishly.
  B. Poverty
  1. The word used for "beggar" in Greek is *ptōchós* (Luke 16:20), from the verb *ptōssō*, "to crouch."
  2. Poor men can only survive by others helping them; hence, they are beggars.

### II. How the Rich Man Lived
  A. He had more than he needed to live on.
  1. He dressed himself in purple.
      *a*) Purple was an expensive dye found in the sac of a rare fish in the Aegean Sea, especially near Thyatira (Acts 16:14; Rev. 18:12). It was a mark of distinction to show he was rich.
      *b*) The verb in Greek is in the imperfect, *enedidúsketo*, "was dressing himself." It was not an occasional affair but a constant custom.
      *c*) He did not have to; he chose to.

2. He dressed himself in fine linen.

    *a)* The word *bússon* is found only here and in Revelation 18:12.

    *b)* It was a type of fine cotton, highly prized by the ancients, especially in Egypt, where they used it to wrap their mummies.

    *c)* This rich man could not wait for his death to use this. He wanted to use it during his life in demonstration of his riches.

B. He was always looking for a good time.

    1. That is what the participle *euphrainómenos* means (Luke 16:19). It is derived from *eú*, an adverb meaning "well" and *phrĕn*, "mind." It means glad-minded, feeling good and having fun.

    2. Life was reduced to uninterrupted fun-making, a constant search for whatever made him feel good.

C. Whatever he did was for vain show.

    1. The English word "sumptuously" in Greek, is *lamprŏs*, "a shining, showing off way." This adverb is used only here and is derived from the verb *lámpō*, "shine," from which our word "lamp" is derived.

    2. The adverb *lamprŏs*, at the end of verse nineteen, indicates his motive of displaying his riches, his fancy clothes, and his merrymaking.

    3. He was a show-off and such a show-off cannot be a Christian, our Lord implies through this story.

D. His heartless, selfish lifestyle was an indication that he was not a believer (Matt. 12:34).

E. The fact that the rich man descended into Hades after death was proof he was not a believer.

    1. The word translated "hell" in verse twenty-three in Greek is *hádēs*, "the place where the disembodied unrighteous go."

    2. It was a place of torture, a place which can be avoided only through transforming, living faith in

Jesus Christ (John 3:18, 36; for the word *hádēs* see Matt. 11:23; Luke 10:15; Acts 2:27, 31).

3. If there is no *hádēs*, "a place of punishment for unbelievers," then Jesus must be a liar! There is *hádēs* because Jesus said there is.

4. There is also a place of rest after death for the believers because Jesus said there is. He called it "Abraham's bosom" because Abraham is considered the patriarch of believers (John 8:39, 56; Acts 3:13, 25; 13:26; Rom. 4:3, 9, 12, 16; Gal. 3:6–9, 16, 18, 29; Heb. 11:8; James 2:21, 23).

## III. How Lazarus Lived

A. "He placed himself."

1. The Greek verb is *ebéblēto* in the pluperfect, which stresses the condition of a past action.

2. It is to be taken rather with the middle meaning and not the passive, indicating Lazarus placed himself at the entrance to the palace of the rich man who was not concerned when he saw the leper's deplorable existence.

B. He was ulcerated.

1. The Greek word is *hēlkōménos* from *hélkos*, ulcer. He was full of ulcers, an indication that he had leprosy.

2. They must have been visible ulcers that should have caused any human being to be moved to compassion. Although this rich man may have been the best dressed, merry-making person, he was not humane.

C. He would have been satisfied with the crumbs which kept falling (*piptónton*) from the rich man's table.

1. Satisfaction with crumbs is characteristic of a believer's life.

2. He did not revolt against the rich man's behavior.

3. He was more humane to the dogs by allowing them to lick his wounds than the rich man ever thought of being to him.

D. Lazarus was truly a believer in spite of his sickness, suffering, and poverty.

1. He died and his soul was tenderly carried, the Greek word indicates, to Abraham's Bosom or Paradise by waiting angels.

2. The prevailing philosophy that believers should be healthy and wealthy is totally erroneous (John 16:33).

3. A Christian has peace not because of health and abundance, but in spite of it.

# The Trinity and the New Birth

Key Verse: John 3:16

---

I. **The Story of Nicodemus Reveals Christ's Divinity**
   A. Nicodemus believed Jesus to be only a teacher (John 3:2) who had, nevertheless, exhibited some signs of divinity.
      1. He conceded that God (*ho Theós*), Jehovah of the Old Testament, must be with Him.
      2. The question he asked himself as he came to visit Jesus was: "Is it possible that Jesus is more than a man?"
   B. Jesus immediately confounded Nicodemus by exposing his ignorance of spiritual matters. In this way, He revealed His true divinity to Nicodemus.
      1. "Jesus answered and said unto him, Verily, verily, I say unto thee, Except a man be born again, he cannot see the kingdom of God" (John 3:3). By these words Jesus indicated that Nicodemus had a need which is common to all men. He showed that only God could fill that void and that He (Jesus) possessed the spiritual insight that Nicodemus lacked (John 3:12).
      2. In verse thirteen Jesus made an even greater revelation about Himself: "And no man hath ascended up to heaven, but he that came down from heaven ['came down' is an aorist participle, indicating the historical moment during which He was conceived through the Holy Spirit (Matt. 1:18, 20)], even the

Son of man which is in heaven." Jesus was referring to Himself, of course, who was simultaneously on earth and in heaven. What is translated, "which is" should rather be "the one being" (*ho ōn*), as in John 1:18. Jesus was declaring that although the incarnation brought Him down to earth, He never ceased being the God of heaven as well.

## II. A Man Can Only Be United to God Through the Action of the Holy Spirit

A. Nicodemus revealed his ignorance of this fact in verse four, ". . . How can a man be born when he is old? can he enter the second time into his mother's womb, and be born?" Nicodemus did not understand the role of the Holy Spirit in uniting a man with God.

B. Jesus explained that there are two births: the physical and the spiritual "That which is born of the flesh [out of the water] is flesh [physical]; and that which is born of the Spirit is spirit [spiritual]."

C. The physical birth of a child involves two human beings, but it was not so with the conception of the Lord Jesus as man. He was born of a woman (Gal. 4:4) through the Holy Spirit (Luke 1:35). Thus, He had man's nature, but without sin (Heb. 4:15), and God's nature combined. He was truly the God-Man, perfect God and perfect Man.

D. Likewise, when a man is born from above, the Holy Spirit is equally involved in converting a sinner into a saint. Although the person continues to be fully man, he also acquires the nature of God (2 Pet. 1:4). As there were two natures in Christ the God-Man, there are two natures in the believer (only Christ, however, was without sin). This spiritual regeneration is only possible for those who first come out of water (a reference to physical birth not water baptism [v. 5]). Pure spiritual beings such as angels are never said to possess or need "the birth from above." It is sinful men that require the new birth.

E. The Holy Spirit must be God come down from heaven, like Jesus (v. 13), in order to have the ability to cause such a spiritual transformation.

F. Jesus also likened the Holy Spirit to the blowing wind: a real presence that cannot be contained. A person knows he is born from above, but he cannot explain or control how the experience took place. Nicodemus was right in expressing wonder. "How can these things be?" (v. 9). Later verses indicate that he too experienced the new birth (John 19:38–42).

## III. God the Father Is Also Involved in the Birth from Above

A. When Nicodemus referred to God, he was thinking of Jehovah of the Old Testament. He did not realize that Jesus and the Holy Spirit were the other two Persons of the Triune God.

B. In His conversation with Nicodemus, Jesus revealed the Trinity. He spoke of God the Father as having loved the world so much that He sent His Son, the second Person of the Trinity, ". . . that whosoever believeth in him should not perish, but have everlasting life" (John 3:16). He reiterated this truth in verse seventeen, "For God [*ho Theós*, 'God the Father'] sent not his Son into the world to condemn the world; but that the world through him might be saved." Thus, it is God the Father who sent God the Son to save the world. God the Holy Spirit effects this salvation in each individual believer's life through the new birth.

# Loving Is Obeying

**Key Verse: John 15:10**

---

**I. Love Is a Magnet**
   A. The Greek word translated "love" in John 15:9 is *agápē*, "unselfish love which seeks to meet a need in another."
      1. Christ wants us to love (*agapáō*) our enemies (Matt. 5:44; Luke 6:27, 35). He does not want us to stay away from them, even as He did not stay aloof from those who hated Him.
      2. He wants us to recognize their need and meet it, even as He met our own need in our sinful condition.
      3. If you are estranged from people, try loving them by meeting a need in their lives. Thus you will build a bridge between you and them.
   B. From *agápē* there springs *philía*, "friendship," which is commonly translated love.
      1. This type of love is based on a relationship of common interests. Two people are friends when they are concerned about the same things. There is more a bond of equality among friends.
      2. The Lord never used the verb *philéō*, "befriend," to tell us to love our enemies. He does not want us to compromise ourselves by associating with those of opposite lifestyles. He does not want us to be unequally yoked with unbelievers (2 Cor. 6:14).
   C. In contrast to *agápē* is the word *érōs* which is "selfish, sexual lust, a desire for someone or something."
      1. This word never occurs in the New Testament.

2. *Érōs* takes, and when what is to be enjoyed no longer satisfies, it is dropped. Erotic marriages end in divorce because they are based not on giving to one another but in receiving.

D. As the magnet attracts that which is opposite to it, so a Holy God draws the sinner to Himself.

II. **The Same Kind of Love Is Extended to Us by Jesus as the Father Extended to Him**

A. "As the Father hath loved me" (John 15:9).

1. The adverb "as" in Greek is *kathōs* from *katá*, "according," and *hōs*, "according as," or in the same manner as.

2. The quality of the love which the Father showed to His only begotten, the unique Son, is the quality of love which the Son demonstrated to us, as branches of His vine.

B. What kind of love was it?

1. It was a love that would not spare Jesus' suffering and death. Jesus had just told His disciples He was going to go away.

2. It was a love that accomplished the Father's purpose, Jesus giving eternal life through His death.

3. The love of the Father did not mean escape from duty, but faithfulness. There was identity of purpose between the Father and the Son.

C. "So have I loved you" (v. 9).

1. The Greek word *kagō* could have been translated "I myself," or "even I myself have loved you."

2. There is no greater love than that between the Father and the Son. Love was not given because the Son needed it, but because of their complete unity of essence, character, and purpose. This is another application of *agapáō*, "living in complete harmony." It is far higher than *philía*, "friendship."

D. The verb "have loved," *ēgápēsa*, in Greek is in the aorist in both phrases.

1. "As the Father hath loved me, so have I loved you." The aorist active means an active voluntary expression of unity of character and purpose between the Father and the Son.

2. It is a historical love. It is sealed and no one can change it. No circumstances in the life of Jesus or the disciples can classify the necessity of suffering by Christ or the disciples as an abandonment. Love does not rescue from suffering but redeems through it.

## III. Obedience Is the Correct Response to Love

A. He who is loved should obey the One who loves him.

B. "Continue ye in my love."

1. "Continue" in Greek is *meínate*, the aorist imperative (John 15:9). It denotes action anchored in love.

2. Each act of obedience to God's commandments makes the relationship firmer.

C. When it comes to Jesus' keeping the Father's commandments, there is no condition—not, "if I keep them," but "I have kept them." Jesus speaks of a completed fact. *Tetḗrēka* is in the perfect tense.

D. Obedience is the secret of abiding in God's love.

# The Coming of the Holy Spirit

Key Verse: John 15:26

---

I. **The Holy Spirit Has Always Existed**
   A. The Lord Jesus has always been. "In the beginning was the Word" (John 1:1) refers to the eternal self-existence of Jesus before He became flesh (John 1:14).
   B. It is equally true that the Holy Spirit has always existed and been active in the affairs of the world along with God the Father, and God the Son. For instance, it was the Holy Spirit who was instrumental in the conception of Jesus in human form (Matt. 1:18, 20). It was also said that John the Baptist would be filled with the Holy Spirit from his mother's womb (Luke 1:15). Likewise, both Zacharias and Elisabeth were filled with the Holy Spirit (Luke 1:41, 67), as were Simeon (Luke 2:25) and Anna (Luke 2:36). These events all occurred before the manifestation of the Holy Spirit at Pentecost.

II. **Jesus Foretold the Coming of the Holy Spirit on the Night Before His Passion**
   A. He presented the Holy Spirit not merely as an energizing power (Luke 4:18; 1 Cor. 3:16; Gal. 4:6), but as a distinct personality, a *paráklētos*, (John 14:16, 26; 15:26; 16:7). In John 16:7 reference is made to <u>Him</u>: "I will send <u>him</u> unto you"; "And when <u>he</u> is come" (v. 8); ". . . when <u>he</u>, the spirit of truth, is come. . ." (v. 13); and "<u>He</u> shall glorify me. . ." (v. 14). Clearly,

43

Christ was predicting the coming of a personal being and not a type of special power.

B. Jesus said in John 15:26, "But when the Comforter is come." The verb used here is *élthē*, the second aorist subjunctive of *érchomai*, indicating a once and for all happening which could be later pinpointed.

## III. The Coming of the Holy Spirit Was a Definite Historical Event

A. He came on the day of Pentecost which was an appointed festival held on the fiftieth day after the beginning of the Passover (Lev. 23:16). Acts 2:1–42 describes in detail His coming to over a hundred disciples and later that day to about three thousand other Jews in Jerusalem.

B. This event also occurred just ten days after Jesus' ascension into heaven (Acts 1:10, 11).

## IV. The Holy Spirit's Coming Initiated the Beginning of the Worldwide Church

A. Before His ascension, Jesus told His disciples that the Holy Spirit would come and empower them to be His witnesses ". . . unto the uttermost part of the earth" (Acts 1:8). John the Baptist had also predicted the coming of the Holy Spirit during his ministry (Matt. 3:11; Mark 1:8; Luke 3:16; John 1:33).

B. The coming of the Holy Spirit abolished the distinctions between Israel and the Gentiles as well as any other human differentiations. Although the event at Pentecost was exclusively for the Jews, the same miraculous signs were later repeated at Caesarea to include Cornelius and others who were Gentiles (Acts 10:44–48; 11:15–18). Then at Ephesus the Holy Spirit also came on those who were calling themselves the disciples of John the Baptist (Acts 19:1–17). On all three of these occasions the one common sign given as evidence of the manifestation of the Holy Spirit was speaking in languages other than their own (Acts 2:4, 6, 8, 11; 10:46; 19:6).

C. This baptism in the Holy Spirit was for the purpose of joining believers to the body of Christ. "For by [in] one Spirit are we all baptized into one body, whether we be Jews or Gentiles, whether we be bond or free; and have been all made to drink into one Spirit" (1 Cor. 12:13). In Jesus, all believers share "One Lord, one faith, one baptism." This baptism is of the Holy Spirit, not water (Eph. 4:5).

D. The Holy Spirit's coming also brought about the full revelation of Jesus Christ. ". . . He shall testify of me" (John 15:26). A testimony (*marturía*) is the making public all that one knows about another. "Howbeit when he, the Spirit of truth, is come, he will guide you into all truth: for he shall not speak of himself; but whatsoever he shall hear, that shall he speak: and he will show you things to come" (John 16:13). "He [himself] shall glorify me: for he shall receive of mine, and shall show it unto you" (John 16:14). Thus, Jesus explains that the Holy Spirit came to teach the believer about Christ and then to unite him with Christ as a member of His body, the Church.

# The Meaning of Pentecost

Key Verse: Acts 2:4

I. The Promise of Baptism in the Holy Spirit
   A. In four instances (Matt. 3:11; Mark 1:8; Luke 3:16; John 1:33) John the Baptist stated that he was baptizing in or with water. After him there was One, Jesus Christ, coming who was stronger and was going to baptize (*baptísei*, future indicative meaning a certain future action) in or with the Holy Spirit.
      1. The baptizer is clearly Jesus Christ.
      2. The element of baptism was going to be the Holy Spirit, even as the element of physical baptism was water.
   B. The purpose of this spiritual baptism is indicated in 1 Corinthians 12:13: "For by [this in Greek is *en*, meaning 'in' or 'with' the Holy Spirit] one Spirit are we all baptized [*ebaptísthēmen*, 'we were all baptized'] into one body [the body of Christ so beautifully described in 1 Cor. 12:14–27], whether we be Jews or Gentiles, whether we be bond or free; and have been all made to drink into one Spirit."
      1. The Holy Spirit must convict the sinner if that conviction is going to be genuine and acceptable to Christ.
      2. There are two instances in the New Testament when human belief was invalid because it was not initiated or energized by the Holy Spirit.
         *a*) Simon the magician believed, but not in the Holy Spirit (Acts 8:9–25). He even fooled Philip the deacon into baptizing him physically with water. This happened in Samaria. Then

there came two apostles, Peter and John. They prayed that those who had believed and were baptized might receive the Holy Spirit and validate their faith. This happened to all of them except Simon, the sorcerer. Only then did these become true believers. Before they simply believed because of the persuasiveness of Philip. Now that their faith was energized by the Holy Spirit, they were truly saved.

*b)* In Acts 19:1–7, we read of some disciples who had believed and experienced the baptism of repentance of John the Baptist, but they had never heard of the Holy Spirit. Therefore, their faith was not energized with the Holy Spirit and was consequently invalid. But when Paul put his hands upon them, they received the Holy Spirit. Their faith was validated, they were truly born again and made fit to become members of the body of Christ.

## II. The Fulfillment of John's Promise of the Baptism in the Holy Spirit

A. The Lord Jesus confirmed and clarified John the Baptist's prediction in Acts 1:5: "For John truly baptized with [or in] water; but ye shall be baptized with [or in] the Holy Ghost not many days hence."

1. The Lord gave further information as to when this historical event was going to take place: "not many days hence." Stated positively, it meant that it would occur shortly. It was an event which indeed occurred ten days after the Lord made this prophesy prior to His ascension. This was the baptism with the Holy Spirit.

2. The expression "baptism" or "baptize in the Holy Spirit," is not found in Acts 2:1–13. How then can we identify this baptism as that to which John the

47

Baptist and Jesus said was yet to come and which Paul said had already taken place (1 Cor. 12:13)?

B. A key occurrence of the term "baptism" or "baptize in the Holy Spirit," found in Acts 11:15, 16, can make this identification clear.

    1. Peter was in Caesarea by the sea speaking to Cornelius and his group of Gentiles. He said, "And as I began to speak, the Holy Ghost fell on them [the Gentiles], as on us [the Jews] at the beginning [*en arché*, which may be understood as the beginning of the body of Christ, the establishment of the Christian church]."

    2. Peter confirms that what the Gentiles witnessed at Caesarea and the Jews witnessed in Jerusalem at Pentecost was the baptism of the Holy Spirit. He said, "Then remembered I the word of the Lord, how that he said, John indeed baptized with water; but ye shall be baptized with the Holy Ghost" (Acts 11:16).

## III. Speaking in Tongues, the Evidence of the Holy Spirit Baptism

A. At Pentecost those Jews who experienced this special coming of the Holy Spirit (see John 14:15–17; 16:7–14) spoke in other (*hétérais*, "qualitatively different" than their mother tongue) languages.

    1. These were not "the unknown tongue" spoken by the Corinthians (1 Cor. 14:2, 4, 13, 19, 26, 27) which was not a language per se, but an utterance not understood by the hearers.

    2. In Acts 2:6, 8 they are definitely called dialects in Greek which can only mean ethnic languages. In other instances, the word *glóssai*, "languages or tongues," is used in the plural with a singular pronoun, referring to ethnic languages (see Mark

16:17; 1 Cor. 12:10, 28, 30; 13:1, 8; 14:5, 6, 18, 22).

B. They needed no interpreter to be understood.

C. They were spoken in the presence of one of the Twelve Apostles, including Paul.

    1. At Pentecost all the apostles were present except Judas.

    2. At Caesarea, Peter was present.

    3. At Ephesus, Paul was present.

D. They spoke as part of a group.

    1. At Pentecost—Jews.

    2. At Caesarea—Gentiles.

    3. At Ephesus—disciples of John the Baptist.

E. In the case of Ephesus in Acts 19:1–7, we don't have the exact expression "baptism" or "baptize in the Holy Spirit," but we do have the speaking in tongues or languages as the evidence of the Holy Spirit baptism. Thus the phenomenon must be identified as the same as at Pentecost and Caesarea.

    1. Therefore, the special coming of the Holy Spirit was the sending of the Paraclete, the Comforter, by the Father and Jesus Christ after His ascension into heaven (John 14:16; 16:16, 17; Acts 1:5).

    2. This does not mean that the Holy Spirit did not exist or was not in the world prior to that time, but at that time He began to be with us as He is now (John 14:17). This period of time in which we are now living is thus the dispensation of the Holy Spirit in a very real sense (John 16:16–20).

## IV. Who Is Baptized with the Holy Spirit?

A. The words of Paul in 1 Corinthians 12:13 make this unmistakably clear, especially if we translate it literally from the Greek: "And indeed in or with one Spirit [that was the event manifested at Jerusalem, Caesarea, and Ephesus] we were all baptized into one body [the body of Christ, the Church], either Jews or Greeks [Gentiles], or slaves or free, and all were given to drink one Spirit" [author's translation].

B. Observe the word *pántes*, "all," occurring twice. Even the immature, carnal Christians of Corinth (1 Cor. 3:1–3) and all true believers whose faith was energized by the Holy Spirit, were baptized into the body of Christ.

C. Clearly this is not an experience of individual believers as a sign of maturity, but it is something Jesus Christ accomplished for us all as a result of His incarnation, crucifixion, resurrection, and ascension. He will finally make the identities of those in His body known at His coming again (Rom. 8:21).

V. **When Does This Baptism in the Holy Spirit Take Place?**

A. Before we are Christians, the Holy Spirit's only relation to us is that He convicts us of sin (John 16:8).

B. Then when we trust the work of Christ for us on the cross, our relation to the Holy Spirit changes (John 14:17; Rom. 8:14).

C. Genuine believers are joined to His body when they are saved. When this joining is done by Christ, it is no more "our" salvation but "His," and once He has made us part of His body no one has the power to tear His body apart by annulling His work.

VI. **Pentecost Is the Beginning of the Baptism in the Holy Spirit, a Work of God Also Manifested at Caesarea and Ephesus**

A. This work of God began the formation of Christ's invisible body, the Church.

B. We personally appropriate this work of Christ when we believe in Christ through the empowering of the Holy Spirit. We can personally experience the meaning of Pentecost today!

# Water Baptism and the Holy Spirit

Key Verse: Acts 8:15

---

I. **Philip Baptized Believers and Unbelievers with Water**
   A. Many in Samaria were baptized after hearing Philip preach about Christ and believing "the things concerning the kingdom of God" (Acts 8:12).
   B. Among them was Simon the magician who had been influencing the people in that region with his magic. Although Simon claimed to be a believer, his heart had not yet been enlightened by the Holy Spirit.

II. **The Apostles Responded to the Situation**
   A. After hearing "that Samaria had received the word of God, they sent unto them Peter and John" (Acts 8:14).
   B. The Apostles' concern was that the believers receive the Holy Ghost (Acts 8:15, 17), the sign of true acceptance by God (Matt. 3:11; Acts 10:44–48).

III. **Water Baptism Is Invalid without the Holy Spirit**
   A. The believers' faith was confirmed and their salvation made sure when they received the Holy Ghost (Acts 8:17; 2 Cor. 1:21, 22; Eph. 1:13, 14).
   B. However, Simon, who observed the proceedings, completely misunderstood their significance. He thought the Holy Ghost was some kind of magical power that could be purchased with money (Acts 8:18, 19).

C. The Apostles rebuked Simon and said that he was still "in the bond of iniquity" and needed to "repent" (Acts 8:22, 23) despite his previous confession and water baptism (Acts 8:13).

D. Jesus had promised that the Holy Ghost would direct His followers into "all truth" (John 16:13). Simon's ignorance of the truth was proof that his heart had not yet been changed by the Holy Ghost and was "not right in the sight of God" (Acts 8:21); water baptism alone had not saved him. Only the Holy Spirit can truly join us to the body of Christ (1 Cor. 12:13).

# God's Spirit in Control of Our Lives

Key Verse: Romans 8:14

---

I. **What Is the Test of a Born-Again Believer?**
   A. One is not marked as a believer by a mere profession of faith, but rather by being indwelt and led by God's Spirit (Rom. 8:11, 14). We are told that the Holy Spirit dwells in us as believers in Christ (Rom. 8:9–11). Paul uses this same idea when he speaks of our being "sealed" by the Holy Spirit (Eph. 1:13; 4:30). We are consequently led by Him (Rom. 8:14).
   B. In Romans 7:17, Paul uses the same words (*oikō en*, "dwell in") to refer to sin dwelling in him as when he speaks of the Spirit dwelling in him (Rom. 8:9). Therefore, Paul is saying that his sinful nature has not been eradicated by the entrance of the Holy Spirit into his life.
   C. Paul desired to serve the indwelling Spirit instead of the sinful flesh which struggled against this (Rom. 7:22, 23).
   D. If he had been led by his old nature, one could question whether he were truly saved. This is confirmed by Romans 8:11, "But if the Spirit of him that raised up Jesus from the dead dwell in you, he that raised up Christ from the dead shall also quicken your mortal bodies by his Spirit that dwelleth in you." The verb for "quicken" is *zōopoiēsei*, "shall make alive." Once we have come to possess spiritual life by means of the implanted Spirit, or after having been "born again"

(John 3:3), it is impossible for the dead flesh to rule over the live Spirit on a permanent basis (1 John 3:6).

## II. The Born-Again Believer Has a Responsibility to Follow the Spirit

A. The Lord does not produce in us a static, dormant stupor when the Spirit enters. In fact, just the opposite occurs; we are immediately called into active combat.

B. "Therefore, brethren, we are debtors, not to the flesh, to live after the flesh" (Rom. 8:12). The expression, "we are debtors" indicates that we are under obligation to God. Because we personally did nothing to merit the indwelling of the Holy Spirit, we are indebted to God for His presence in our lives. The way we repay God for His grace is to follow after the Spirit and not the flesh.

## III. There Are Inevitable Consequences of Our Lifestyles

A. Paul declares in Romans 8:13, 14 that our way of life clearly demonstrates whether we have been born again into God's family.

B. "If ye live after the flesh, ye shall die" (Rom 8:13). Such a person clearly does not have the Spirit in him and will be eternally separated from God, no matter what profession of faith he makes. He is excluded because his life yields the fruits of the flesh (Gal. 5:19–21).

C. Those who follow the Spirit, on the other hand, grow from the immature state of childhood (*tékna*, "children" [John 1:12]) to the maturity of sonship (*huioí*, "sons" [Rom. 8:14]), who as grown-ups voluntarily conform to Jesus Christ. Their conformity to Christ confirms that they were indeed born again and are "joint-heirs" with Christ. In Romans 8:16 the word "children" is used: "The Spirit itself beareth witness with our spirit, that we are the children [*tékna*] of God." *Téknon* means "one born," thus, it refers to the new birth (John 1:12). Afterwards, however, comes the maturation process. This growth into sonship is achieved by means of obedience to the Holy Spirit in our lives (Rom. 8:14) and God's will for us (Eph. 2:10).

# No One Can Separate Us From God's Love

Key Verse: Romans 8:31

---

### I. Is God for Us?

A. Sometimes we may think that a certain influential person would be willing to help us anytime, but then in a time of need we discover this is not true.

B. Our assurance of God's love, on the other hand, is dependent upon our relationship with Him and knowledge of His faithfulness. If we are strangers to Him, then we will resent any interference in our lives. But if He is our Father, we will desire to be close to Him. If God seems to be far away, it is because we have moved away from Him and not vice versa. We must remain in fellowship with God in order to realize His faithfulness to us.

C. In Romans 8:31 the phrase "If God be for us" is poorly translated. The particle *ei* does not provide for a supposition, but for a certainty. It is not a condition, but a conclusion. It should really read, "since God is for us." Because it is certain that God is for us, the conclusion follows, "who can be against us?"

### II. Can God Forsake Us?

A. All believers can trust their omnipotent, omniscient, and all-loving God to never forsake them. This is the Apostle Paul's whole argument in Romans 8:31–38. God, who demonstrated His love, knowledge, and power so definitively and tangibly, can also certainly be trusted to keep us victorious and safe from all dangers, external and internal. Furthermore, He who was willing to give the ultimate gift of His Son to die for us, "how shall he not with him also freely give us all things?" (Rom. 8:32). Will He allow anything or anyone to snatch us from His hands (John 10:28, 29) after paying so dear a price?

B. Just as we did not earn salvation, we cannot earn His protection. This is indicated by the two verbs used in Romans 8:32: *parédoken*, "he delivered him up," and *charísetai*, "freely give." The verb *charísetai* is the future indicative of *charízomai*, "to give as a matter of favor, not as a deserved payment for what one has done." God's preserving believers is based on our justification. But we must always remember that grace also causes us to receive a new nature so that we can perform works of righteousness. Thus there are two parallel truths at work here:

1. God imputes righteousness to us despite the fact that we do not have any good works of our own (Rom. 4:6; Titus 3:5).

2. God remakes us "unto good works" (1 Cor. 1:30; 2 Cor. 9:10; Eph. 2:10; 5:9; 1 John 3:7, 10). The verb *charísetai*, being in the future indicative, means that He "will freely give" us what we need each time an occasion arises. We do not receive all His grace at once. When He brings us into a situation or permits us to be in one, He gives the necessary grace and gifts to face it.

## III. God Guarantees Grace to Us

A. Paul lists some of the situations where God's grace is sufficient. One such circumstance is being falsely accused of not being genuine believers. The only opinion we should value in this regard is that of God himself, for "It is God that justifieth" (Rom. 8:33).

B. Tribulation from outside circumstances (*thlípsis*), inner depression (*stenochōría* translated "distress"), persecution, famine, nakedness, peril, and the sword shall never separate us from the love of God (Rom. 8:35).

C. Paul ends with a superlative list of obstacles: ". . . neither death, nor life, nor angels, nor principalities, nor powers, nor things present, nor things to come, nor height, nor depth, nor any other creature. . ." (Rom. 8:38). He assures us that none of these extremes will ever be able to separate us from the "love of God" which is rooted in Christ Jesus our Lord (Rom. 8:39).

# The Mystery of Christmas

Key Verse: Romans 16:25

---

I. **What Is a Mystery?**
   A. The word "mystery" is the Greek word, *mustérion*, derived from the Greek verb *muéō*, "to initiate." It is also related to *múō* meaning "to shut the eyes or the mouth." Consequently, it stands for rites and truths which must be closely guarded by those who possess them.
   B. The meaning of this word in Classical Greek was "anything hidden or secret." In the plural, *tá mustéria*, "the sacred rites," it denoted secrets which were kept from the uninitiated.
   C. In the New Testament, it is the unrevealed that is mysterious. Many now see "through a glass, darkly" (1 Cor. 13:12) and only "know in part" (1 Cor. 13:9). When we reach heaven, we shall know in full, even as we are known (1 Cor. 13:12; 1 John 3:2).
   D. The revelation of the coming of Jesus Christ into the world is not only an historical fact to be learned, but a spiritual truth that only God through the Holy Spirit can reveal to our hearts.

II. **Christmas Presents Two Great Mysteries**
   A. The first is the fact of the incarnation of the Word, *Lógos*, or "intelligence" (John 1:1, 14). This mystery is incomprehensible to our human minds. How can the infinite, eternal Spirit take upon Himself a tangible form (*morphēn*, Phil. 2:6–8)? Jesus Christ partially revealed this mystery to some in His day and continues

to do so in ours (Eph. 3:4; 5:32; 6:19; Col. 4:3). Those who understand the mystery of Christ's birth are the initiates who now have access to further secrets of the kingdom of God (Matt. 13:11; Mark 4:11; Luke 8:10). These believers try to pass on the mystery of Christ and His kingdom (1 Cor. 2:7; Eph. 6:19; Col. 2:2), but to those unenlightened by God Himself it is all foolishness (1 Cor. 2:14).

B. After "the Word was made flesh," He "dwelt among us" (John 1:14). What is translated as "among" is the Greek preposition *en*, which can mean "among" but primarily means "in." Indeed, the second Christmas miracle is even greater. God not only came "among us" but He actually dwells "in" us. When He does, we in effect become members of His body, the Church, and are initiated into all of the privileges thereof.

## III. What Does Christmas Mean to Us?

A. First, we must accept it as a mystery (Rom. 16:25); otherwise we will underestimate its value. The more mysterious God is, the more glorious He is in our eyes (Prov. 25:2; 1 Cor. 2:7). It is a humbling experience when we must confess that we neither know nor understand something, and that no matter how hard we try, we cannot change this.

B. Jesus Christ is also able to "establish" us (Rom. 16:25). The word for establish is *stērixai*, the aorist infinitive of *stērizō*, "to make steadfast, to cause us to stand and to keep us from evil" (see 1 Thess. 3:13; 2 Thess. 2:17; 3:3; 1 Pet. 5:10). Once we are initiated into the revelation of His mystery, we in Christ and He in us, nothing will be able to move us (John 10:28, 29). It is He who has the power (*dunaménō*) to stabilize us in the faith once and for all.

C. Paul personally appropriated this good news for himself, which is why he referred to it as "my gospel."

Likewise, it must become personal to each one of us.

D. That which was good news for Paul became "the preaching of Jesus Christ" to others (Rom. 16:25). He never attempted to make Christ's incarnation understandable; instead he preached that it must be accepted as true. When believed and acted upon, this mystery is indeed revolutionary.

E. We should count ourselves privileged that the wonderful mystery which remained silent (*sesigēménou*, the perfect passive participle of *sigáō*) "since the world began" (Rom. 16:25) has now been entrusted to us, not only for our own good, but also for the good of those with whom we share it.

F. The purpose of God revealing Christ to us is so that we might obey Him through faith (Rom. 16:26). This devotion to Christ is His plan for us and the people of all nations. In His wisdom, God planned this great mystery for His own glory (Rom. 16:27) which is revealed in us and others to come.

# Warnings to Modern Day "Corinthians"

Key Verse: 1 Corinthians 10:11

## I. Corinth Was a Prosperous, but Sin-Filled City

A. Paul did not hesitate to come and preach the gospel in such an environment proving that "where sin abounded, grace did much more abound" (Rom. 5:20).

B. People living in such a sinful environment today also need the same four exhortations Paul gave to the Corinthian Christians (1 Cor. 10:7–10).

## II. Beware of Idolatry

A. "Neither be ye idolaters" (1 Cor. 10:7). The verb translated "be ye" is *ginesthe* meaning, "keep becoming." There is an insidiousness about idolatry as we tend to conform to the values of our society.

B. Paul uses the illustration of the Israelites in the wilderness where they "offered burnt offerings, and brought peace offerings: and the people sat down to eat and to drink, and rose up to play" (Ex. 32:6). The Israelites imitated the false worship of the peoples around them rather than waiting for Moses to come down from the mountain with God's instructions.

## III. Beware of Fornication

A. "Neither let us commit fornication" (1 Cor. 10:8). The verb is in the present subjunctive which indicates continuous action. Again, our culture is inundated with sexual messages urging constant gratification.

B. Paul refers to the time of Israel's stay in Shittim where the men were enticed by the women of Moab into committing fornication with them and later idolatry as well (Num. 25:1, 2).

IV. **Beware of a Complaining Attitude**
   A. "Neither let us tempt Christ" (1 Cor. 10:9). The verb *ekpeirázōmen* is also in the present subjunctive, warning us against constantly complaining.
   B. When Israel blamed God and Moses for their poor diet in the wilderness, many were destroyed by "fiery serpents" (Num. 21:4–6). Paul says these lessons are for our good as well (1 Cor. 10:11).

V. **Beware of a Spirit of Dissatisfaction**
   A. "Neither murmur ye" (1 Cor. 10:10). The verb is *goggúzete* in the present imperative meaning "to manifest sullen discontent."
   B. Because of Israel's negative attitude toward God in the wilderness despite His provision for them, God allowed none of them to go into the Promised Land except Caleb, Joshua, and those under twenty years of age (Num. 14:22–30). What an admonition to Christians today!

# Victory over Temptation

Key Verse: 1 Corinthians 10:13

---

I. **How Is Temptation Presented in the New Testament?**
A. The word in Greek is *peirasmós* derived from *peíra*, "experience" (Heb. 11:29, 36). The verb is *peírō*, "to pierce through with a weapon or spear." Intransitively it means "to pass through." As a verb, *peírō* does not occur in the New Testament, but the verb *peirázō*, "to tempt," is used with the following meanings.
1. To try, to prove in a good sense (John 6:6; 2 Cor. 13:5; Heb. 11:17) or a bad sense (Matt. 16:1; 22:18, 35; 1 Cor.10:9).
2. To tempt by soliciting to sin (Matt. 4:1; 1 Thess. 3:5; James 1:13, 14).
    *a*) In this sense we have Satan called "the tempter" (Matt. 4:3; 1 Thess. 3:5). Satan tries to prove one has been evil.
       (1) Satan has a particular interest in discrediting believers.
       (2) He tries to entangle us in sin, and thereby prove us to be sinful. His temptation, if not resisted, causes us to do that which we know is contrary to God's will.
    *b*) Satan's temptation is always for the purpose of causing us to fail.
       (1) He wants to confuse believers and cause them to stumble; if we mistakenly believe that salvation leads to sinlessness, this will prove to us that we are not what we believe God made us to be.

(2) Satan further intends that any failures on our part will lead us to think that God is powerless to meet our needs. He desires us to forget that any failure comes from our refusal to meet God's conditions, and not from any limitation on God's part.

3. Temptation is said to be initiated by God in several Scriptures. This is temptation in the sense of testing.

   *a*) God uses testing to prove what He made us to be and to give us the satisfaction of victory. When God tempts us, it is for the purpose of proving us in order to promote us.

   *b*) This use of temptation is equivalent to testing a child—it is not for the purpose of failing him, but for the purpose of preparing him to receive more advanced knowledge.

B. Why did the Lord teach us to pray that God would not lead us into temptation?

   1. The word for "lead" is *eisenégkes* meaning "bring us into." In other words we should pray, "Do not lead us into a path which will allow us to be tempted by the devil."

   2. It is an acknowledgment of our weakness in handling Satan. Jesus knows that we are better off resisting the devil so that he will flee from us (James 4:7). When it comes to Satan we must humbly confess we cannot handle him on our own.

C. But how can we account for the statements in James 1:12–15?

   1. "Blessed is the man that endureth temptation" (James 1:12).

      *a*) "Blessed" is *makários* which means "indwelt by God, and because of it, fully satisfied." A person "blessed" in this sense will not be overcome by any testing which God permits or directs. Such testing for them leads to demonstrating that they are approved before God.

b) This is *dokimé*, "testing in the positive sense." The second part of the verse makes it clear: "For when he [the blessed person] is tried, he shall receive the crown of life."

2. God does not tempt us to cause us to sin. Only Satan or our lustful desires do that. Hence the statement:

a) "Let no man say when he is tempted, I am tempted of God: for God cannot be tempted with evil, neither tempteth he any man" (James 1:13)

b) God does not tempt (test) us to give us an opportunity to sin, but to give us an opportunity to show ourselves approved. Our Adamic nature causes us to misunderstand God's purposes in the circumstances He permits us to go through.

## II. What Is the Temptation "Common to Man" (1 Cor. 10:13)?

A. James acknowledged that temptation to sin springs from within our Adamic nature (James 1:14).

B. Paul acknowledges that temptation which may result in sin may also be due to temptations surrounding us. That is the temptation "common to man." In Greek it is *anthrópinos*, "human, pertaining to man." As long as we are human beings living in an unredeemed creation (Rom. 8:19–23), we shall experience human temptations.

C. Such temptations pursue us.

1. We should not pursue them.

2. We must not flirt with temptation.

3. The verb "hath taken," *eiléphen* in Greek, is the active voice of *lambánō*, "to take, to reach us and

take hold of us." This means that temptation is in pursuit of the saint who is on the move for God.

D. Such temptation pertaining to our humanity is never beyond our strength to bear and overcome. God will not allow us to be tempted beyond our strength.

E. God is faithful, *pistós*, "dependable." He will give us the strength to overcome. We cannot do it on our own.

F. Such temptations are not caused by God directly, but they are part and parcel of our temptable yet unredeemed bodies and the unredeemed creation. They are the result of Adam's sin, and yet God promises victory as we experience the temptations of our fallen humanity.

G. He promises "a way of escape." The Greek word is *ékbasis* which occurs only here in 1 Corinthians 10:13 and Hebrews 13:7. It is derived from the preposition *ek*, "out of," and *baínō*, "to go, proceed." It refers to what is to come out of a certain situation. It actually does not mean a way of escape, if by that we are to understand it as merely getting out of the situation, but rather it means that something is going to come out of it, that God in His faithful dependability is going to enrich our experience by any situation that tempts us. God never permits anything in our lives without a purposeful end (Rom. 8:28).

H. Knowing this makes every temptation involved in our humanity bearable as the last phrase states: "that ye may be able to bear it."

# Confirmed Hope

Key Verse: 1 Corinthians 15:20

---

## I. Life Without Hope is Worthless

A. Hope must be grounded upon something, for baseless hope is the product of an irrational mind.

B. It should involve not only this life, but also the life that follows death (1 Cor. 15:19).

C. If we hope only for what death will eventually terminate anyway, we are more miserable than all men. This means that we as believers must have hope beyond the grave.

## II. Christ Is Not Only for This Life

A. Certainly, Paul's concern was that Christ be magnified in his body (Phil. 1:20).

B. However, to be absent from the body meant that he would be with Christ (Phil. 1:23) in an even greater state of existence.

## III. Christ's Resurrection Is the Foundation of Our Hope

A. Paul gave historical proof of Christ's physical resurrection (1 Cor. 15:4–11).

B. He also countered the possible objections to Christ's resurrection (1 Cor. 15:12–18). No such argument can stand before the historical fact of Christ's resurrection. "But now is Christ risen from the dead" (1 Cor. 15:20). The perfect middle deponent verb *egḗgertai* means that Christ raised Himself and He is alive today. Christ is God who became man, yet never ceased to be God (Phil. 2:6–8), who died, and who rose again. Thus, He became "the firstfruits of them that slept," or who have died (1 Cor. 15:20).

IV. **Because He Raised Himself, He Will Also Raise Us**
   A. The word *aparchē* means the firstfruit, the beginning fruit, one who starts. Because He rose, He will raise us too.
   B. His assertions about our resurrection are trustworthy (John 5:25; 11:25; 1 Thess. 4:13–17).

# Christ Makes Us New Creatures

Key Verse: 2 Corinthians 5:17

---

I. **What Is the Natural Man Like?**
   A. The natural man does not perceive God (Rom. 8:7).
   B. Consequently, he cannot please God (Rom. 8:8).

II. **It Is Christ Who Makes the Difference**
   A. Christ must actually indwell us (John 17:23, 26; Rom. 8:10; Gal. 2:20; Col. 1:27).
   B. It is only when Christ is in us that we become acceptable to God (Rom. 8:1; 1 Cor. 1:30).
   C. In this state, nothing can separate us from God's love (Rom. 8:38, 39).

III. **Christ Enters Us Because of Our Faith in Him**
   A. Christ and the prophets before Him proclaimed that He was the way to salvation (Is. 53:11; Matt. 3:11; John 5:24; 10:9; 11:25; 14:6).
   B. The apostles also preached salvation through faith in Christ alone (Rom. 10:8–11; Eph. 2:8).

IV. **Those in Christ Are Changed People**
   A. Paul used the Greek word *kainē*, which means qualitatively new (2 Cor. 5:17). No one can be in Christ without being radically changed.
   B. This transformation is also called *katallagē*, "reconciliation" (Rom. 5:10; 2 Cor. 5:18–20). We change from being an enemy of God to becoming a friend (Rom. 5:10).

70

C. The old nature is being "crucified" or put to death (Rom. 6:6).

D. Likewise, John says, "Whosoever abideth in him sinneth not . . ." (1 John 3:6). The verb is in the durative present, meaning habitually. However, if we commit a single sin (*hamárte*), "we have an advocate with the Father, Jesus Christ the righteous" (1 John 2:1).

V. **"Old Things Are Passed Away; Behold, All Things Are Become New"**

A. The word used for "old" is *archaía*, "original," and not simply *palaiá*, "old." Original sin has been done away with by Christ's death on the cross (Heb. 10:10).

B. The verb "passed away" is *parélthen*, meaning "gone forever."

C. Then the exclamation "behold" indicates surprise and delight at the total change which has taken place in the believer.

D. "All things are become new." The verb *gégonen* is in the perfect tense which indicates that things not only became new in the past, but continue to become new in the present.

E. Furthermore, the change is all-inclusive (*tá pánta*), each individual thing and all of them collectively become new in the life of the Christian as he sees things in relation to Jesus as his Savior and Lord.

# How to Live Victoriously In an Evil World

Key Verse: Galatians 1:4

---

I. **The World in Which We Live Today Is Evil**
   A. The world was not always evil.
      1. The creation narrative many times states that what God made was good (Gen. 1:4, 12, 18, 21, 25, 31).
      2. The world became evil through man's disobedience to God (Gen. 3).
      3. In Greek the most common word for the world is *kósmos*, "the sum total of the material universe, including man." *Kósmos* is derived from the verb *kosméō*, "to beautify," which indicates the original creation and purpose of the world. It was good. But since the fall of man, the good and beauty in the world can best be discerned and enjoyed by those who have God within them. These are the blessed and the meek which are described in the third beatitude (Matt. 5:5). They are the ones who inherit the earth, who enjoy its original purpose.
      4. The Greek word, however, in Galatians 1:4 is *aiōn*, which means "age, generation, or a kind of people" (Matt. 13:22; Luke 16:8; 20:34; 1 Cor. 1:20; Eph. 2:2; 1 Tim. 6:17; 2 Tim. 4:10; Titus 2:12).
   B. This generation of evil will continue only for a time.
      1. Jesus did not come the first time to put an end to this generation.
      2. Jesus will put an end to it at a specific time in the future when He will come again in His glory. For

this reason Paul calls the current time "this present evil world."

a) The first time Christ came as a Lamb to take away the sin of the world (*kósmou*, the people within this *aiōn*, "generation, time frame"). See John 1:29, 36; Acts 8:32; 1 Peter 1:19.

(1) He saves individuals within this world (*kósmos*) and time (*aiōn*), but He does not take them out of the world (see John 17:6, 9, 12–20; 1 Cor. 5:9, 10).

(2) He preserves the redeemed in the world during this age (1 Pet. 1:5).

b) He will come again to judge the world (Matt. 25:31–46; Acts 10:42; 17:31; 24:25; Rev. 20:11–15).

(1) This will be the consummation of the age (*suntéleia toú aiōnos*, often wrongly translated as "the end of the world." See Matt. 13:39, 40, 49; 24:3; Heb. 9:26).

(2) When this present age is consummated, there will be a new age. This is designated as "the age coming," *ho aiōn ho erchómenos*, meaning "the next life" (Mark 10:30; Luke 18:30) in contrast to "this age," *ho aiōn hoútos* (Matt. 13:22; Luke 16:8; 20:34; 1 Cor. 1:20; 2:6; Gal. 1:4; Eph. 2:2; 1 Tim. 6:17; 2 Tim. 4:10; Titus 2:12).

(3) At that time our human bodies will be changed (Rom. 8:23; 1 Cor. 15:20–22, 51–55; 1 Thess. 4:14–17), and so will the whole universe (Rom. 8:19–23; Rev. 21:1).

## II. Christ's Death Saves Us from Sin While We Are Still in This Evil World (Gal. 1:4)

A. Christ's death was a voluntary gift: "Who gave himself." His love for us prompted Him to give Himself for us while we were still ungodly enemies of God and at home in this evil world (Rom. 5:6–8).

B. Christ's death was necessary because of our sin. This can be seen by considering what "for" means in the sentence, "He died for our sins."

1. He died in behalf of or because of our sins. This is the basic meaning of the preposition *hupér*, translated "for." When He did that, our sins were removed from us once and for all. They were buried in the depths of the sea, so to speak (Mic. 7:19). He forgave our sins. The word "forgive" in Greek is *aphíēmi*, "to send away from us." The death of Christ thus deals first with our sins by removing them from us.

2. He gave His own body, voluntarily accepting death for the sake of our own dead bodies. Our bodies were dead because of sin (Eph. 2:1). Moreover, with His own resurrection, He also raises unto newness of life all those who believe on Him. Ephesians 2:5 states it clearly: "Even when we were dead in sins, hath quickened us together with Christ (by grace ye are saved)." That word translated "quickened together" is *sunezōopoiēse*; He gave His life to simultaneously give us the life of His resurrection. See also Colossians 2:13.

3. Thus, Jesus through His death and resurrection took away our sins and endowed us with His life.

4. This achieved our justification before God. When Christ presents the believer to the Father and declares that His offer has been accepted by the sinner through the convicting power of the Holy Spirit, then the Father declares the sinner free of guilt. He is then justified and acquires peace with God and access to God (Rom. 5:1; Gal. 2:16). At

the time the sinner is changed to a new creature, he or she becomes just. He acquires God's righteousness and His nature (2 Cor. 5:21).

C. If we do not recognize our sinfulness, His death for us is ineffective. My recognition of the fact that I am a sinner is absolutely necessary if Christ's death is to obtain salvation for me.

III. **Accepting Christ's Death and His Salvation Leads to a Life of Constant Struggle in This Sinful and Evil World**

A. When Christ removes our sins, He changes us completely (2 Cor. 5:17).

   1. But the world and age in which we must remain continues to be the old, fallen, unredeemed world (*kósmos*) and age (*aiōn*).

   2. They will not change until Jesus comes to reign forever and ever. That expression "forever and ever" is *aiōnes aiōnōn*, "the ages of the ages," and it means interminable or interminably (see Gal. 1:5; Phil. 4:20; 1 Tim. 1:17; 2 Tim. 4:18; Heb. 13:21; 1 Pet. 4:11; 5:11; Rev. 1:18; 4:9, 10; 5:13, 14; 7:12; 10:6; 11:15; 14:11; 15:7; 19:3; 20:10; 22:5).

B. Christ's sacrifice can deliver the believer from the spirit of this evil age. This is clearly stated as one of the purposes of Christ's death, "that he might deliver us [the believers] from this present evil world [*aiōnos*, 'age']" (Gal. 1:4).

   1. This does not mean that He takes us away physically from the world, but He gives us victory against sin while we are in an age permeated with evil. We can be <u>in</u> the world, but not <u>of</u> the world as our Lord prayed in John 17:15 in His high-priestly prayer (John 17:9–18): "I pray not that thou shouldest take them out of the world, but that thou shouldest keep them from the evil."

2. This "present age" represents the philosophy of life of this age and it is evil. The Greek word for evil is *ponērós*, "malevolent."

3. "According to the will of God and our Father" (Gal. 1:4).

   *a)* The will of God is always that we may not be affected by any worldly philosophy of life.

   *b)* Although we are surrounded by evil, God should never be blamed for it. We are reaping the consequences of our inherited and personal sin.

   *c)* In spite of all the evil that surrounds us, God is still our Father and He will fully protect us while we are in the world and on our way out.

# The True Gospel and Another Gospel

Key Verse: Galatians 1:8

---

I. **What Is the True Gospel?**
   A. The "good news," *euaggélion*, is for all (John 1:12; 3:16; 1 Tim. 4:10; 1 John 2:2).
   B. It is good news because it offers us what we need—grace, undeserved favor—and not what we deserve. Twice the word grace is mentioned in this passage (Gal. 1:3, 6).
   C. Christ offers this grace, not as a mere man, but as an equal with God. Notice verse three, "Grace be to you, and peace, from God the Father, and from our Lord Jesus Christ." He is not presented here as Savior only, but also as Lord. If He is not received as Lord, neither can He be received as Savior.
   D. It is good news because it gives us peace. When we appropriate the grace which comes from God the Father and the Lord Jesus, we experience reconciliation with God and the resulting peace brings abundant harmony.

II. **The Gospel Signifies What Christ Did for Us**
   A. "Who gave himself for our sins" (Gal. 1:4). Christ's gift was both voluntary and undeserved. It cannot become ours, however, until we confess our sinfulness (Matt. 3:2; Rom. 3:23; 1 John 1:9) and turn to Christ for salvation (Acts 2:38; Rom. 10:9, 10).
   B. When we trust Him, Christ delivers us from this present evil world (Gal. 1:4). *Exéletai*, "that He might

deliver us," is derived from the preposition *ek* or *ex*, "out of," and *airéō*, "to take." It is in the subjunctive aorist, indicating a definite act of rescue. In spite of the fact that we, as salt and light (Matt. 5:13, 14; John 17:6–16), still remain in the world, Christ removes its evil influence from us.

III. **What Is a False Gospel?**

    A. Any teaching about Christ that denies the following basic facts is "another gospel" (Gal. 1:6):

        1. ". . . Christ died for our sins according to the Scriptures" (1 Cor. 15:3).

        2. "He was buried, and . . . rose again the third day according to the Scriptures" (1 Cor. 15:4).

        3. "Who is a liar but he that denieth that Jesus is the Christ?" (1 John 2:22). It is a false gospel when it is based only on the humanity of Jesus. The Lord Jesus must be believed in as the God-Man.

    B. Any belief which suggests works to be the means of salvation is not the gospel. By faith we receive what Christ accomplished for us as a gracious gift (Rom. 5:1; 10:17; Gal. 2:16; Eph. 2:8, 9).

    C. Finally, a "gospel" which does not produce a changed life is false (James 1:22; 2:14, 17, 18). There must be a transformation in the life of the one believing the gospel, or else that gospel is *héteron*, "another of a different kind" (Gal. 1:6), and not *állos*, "another" which could qualify as the gospel. A believer in the true gospel becomes alienated from the world system (John 15:18–25; 17:14; 1 John 2:15; 3:13) while demonstrating the love of God to all those around (1 John 3:10, 14, 23; 4:7, 8, 11, 12, 19–21; 5:2).

# The Ineffectiveness of the Law to Save or Sanctify

Key Verse: Galatians 2:16

---

I. **The Jews Considered the Gentiles to Be Sinners While Exempting Themselves from Such Condemnation**
   A. Paul rejects such a principle. No one can claim righteousness merely because of ancestry, even Jewish (Rom. 2:1–3, 17).
   B. Because the Jews had been given the Law, their sinfulness became even more evident (Rom. 7:7–12).
   C. The Jews needed to believe on the Lord Jesus for forgiveness of their sins just as much as the Gentiles. In Galatians 2:15 Paul refers to this fact, "We being Jews by nature and not sinners from among the Gentiles" (author's translation), meaning that they were sinners as well as the Gentiles.

II. **Both Jews and Gentiles Are Justified by Faith in Jesus Christ**
   A. Paul emphasizes three times in Galatians 2:16 that it is not "by the works of the law" that we are justified before God.
   B. This verse begins with the participle *eidótes*, "knowing." *Oída*, from which *eidótes* is derived, refers to instinctive, intuitive knowledge. No one has to teach us that we are unacceptable to God (James 5:6). Because of His justice, God cannot be a respecter of persons. He judges all equally by His law (Acts 10:34; Rom. 2:11; Eph. 6:9; Col. 3:25; James 2:1).

C. Thus, both Jews and Gentiles as lawbreakers can be declared just only through faith in Jesus Christ (Acts 4:12; 16:30, 31; Rom. 5:9; 10:9).

III. **Faith Is Not Only the Basis of Justification but of Sanctification as Well**

A. The Judaizers had been teaching that after being justified by Christ, the believers must again put themselves under the Mosaic Law to achieve righteousness (Gal. 2:17, 18).

B. Paul argues that Christ is not a "minister of sin" (v. 17). In other words, He is not responsible for our continuing sin after we are justified by faith.

C. The answer to this dilemma is not to again put ourselves under the Law but to continue on in our new life of faith in Christ (Gal. 2:20). His sacrifice has made the Law completely useless in achieving sanctification for the believer.

# What Was the Function of the Law?

Key Verse: Galatians 3:24

---

I. **The Mosaic Law Functioned as a Schoolmaster**
   A. It taught the Jews their sinfulness and need of a Savior (Gal. 3:24).
   B. It functioned from the time of Moses "till the seed [Christ] should come" (Gal. 3:19).
   C. The coming of Christ terminated the Law for both Jews and Gentiles (Gal. 3:8, 9). Paul defines Christ's coming as the arrival of the faith (*hē pístis*). Abraham had subjective faith in God's promise until Christ became the object of that faith or "the faith."

II. **The Law Kept the Jews under Guard**
   A. The function of the Law is indicated by the verb *ephrouroúmetha*, "were kept under" (KJV); "kept in custody" (NASV); "were held prisoners" (NIV). Actually the Greek word *phroúreō* means "to keep guard." The Jews were protected from sin by means of the Law. They tried to avoid disobeying God's specific commands. It provided obedience of the letter, not the spirit of the Law.
   B. While the Jews were guarded by the Law, however, they were also its prisoners. They could not approach God except by the provisions given by Moses.

## III. Christ Liberates Us from the Law and Its Effects

A. Christ achieved the perfection demanded by the Law, and thereby, freed us from the consequences of our disobedience (Gal. 3:13; 5:1).

B. When Christ lives in us and our wills are conformed to His, we are liberated from the power of sin over us (Rom. 8:1). Through faith in Christ, we may achieve true freedom (Rom. 8:2, 4; Gal. 5:16).

# How to Walk as Children of Light

Key Verse: Ephesians 5:8

I. We Are to Realize the Change Produced in Us When We Turned to Christ (Eph. 5:8)

    A. "Ye were sometime in darkness." The word *skótos* is used metaphorically here. The other two words for darkness, *skótia*, "the result of darkness" and *zóphos*, "thick darkness, the gloom of the underworld"), are used, as in Hebrews 12:18; 2 Peter 2:4, 17; and Jude 1:6, 13.

        1. In the Old Testament, darkness is used to depict man's moral depravity (Prov. 2:13; Is. 5:20; 60:2) and in the New Testament it is the emblem of sin as a state of spiritual ignorance (Matt. 4:16; 6:23; Luke 1:79; 11:35; 22:53; John 1:5; 3:19; 8:12; 12:35, 46; Acts 26:18; Rom. 2:19; 13:12; 1 Cor. 4:5; 2 Cor. 6:14; Eph. 5:8, 11; 6:12; Col. 1:13; 1 Thess. 5:4, 5; 1 Pet. 2:9; 1 John 1:5, 6; 2:8, 9, 11).

        2. Darkness also stands for the desolation of divine punishment (Matt. 8:12; 22:13; 25:30; 2 Pet. 2:17; Jude 1:6, 13). When Paul says "you were in darkness," he means not only that they were in sin, but that they were worthy of punishment because of it.

    B. Paul urges us to realize what we are now.

        1. "But now are ye light in the Lord" (Eph. 5:8). A look at the past helps us to understand the difference Christ has made in our lives as we compare

our former sinful desires to our regenerated heart (1 Pet. 2:9; 1 John 2:8).

2. What precisely does it mean to be in the light?

   *a)* Light in the Old Testament often denotes a state of life as opposed to death (Job 33:28, 30; Ps. 56:13).

   *b)* Light portrays the salvation and blessing which God gives to His people (Ps. 4:6; 27:1; 36:9; 43:3; Is.10:17; Mic. 7:8; Acts 26:18). In Hebrews *phōtisthéntes*, or "enlightened ones," denotes those who had the experience of salvation (Heb. 6:4; 10:32).

   *c)* Light also symbolizes moral purity. "God is light, and in him is no darkness at all" (1 John 1:5), where darkness represents sin (1 Thess. 5:5).

## II. Being in the Light Involves Moral Responsibilities and Opportunities

A. Our responsibilities are expressed as a command to "Walk as children of light."

1. Walking is commonly used as a figure of speech for Christian conduct (Rom. 6:4; 2 Cor. 5:7).

2. Walking indicates forward motion. The Christian standard is not attained at once (Phil. 3:12).

3. There is a certain destination and predetermined road that those who are in the light ought to follow.

   *a)* The Greek word which is translated "walk" is *stoichéō* from *stoichós*, "a row" (Acts 21:24; Rom. 4:12; Gal. 5:25; 6:16; Phil. 3:16). It simply means to advance in rows, in an orderly fashion as opposed to the verb *peripatéō*, which means "to walk about."

   *b)* The word *stoichéō* is also used in Galatians 5:25, "If we live in the Spirit, let us also walk [*stoichō-men*] in the Spirit." It is the Spirit who indicates the pathway we should follow. In Galatians 6:16 Paul says: "And as many as walk [*stoichḗsousin*] according to this rule, peace be on them, and mercy. . . ." In Philippians 3:16 he also declares ". . . let us walk [*stoichein*] by the same rule, let us mind the same thing."

4. In the Christian life there must be rules and thoughts common to all Christians. If we find ourselves all alone doing whatever we wish, there may be shadows obscuring our light.

B. Fulfilling our responsibility to walk in the light of God's Word gives us the opportunity to produce the fruit of the Spirit.

1. Fruitfulness is what the Lord desires from our walk in Him as shown in the parable of the wicked vine dressers (Matt. 21:33–46; Mark 12:1–12; Luke 20:9–19), the parable of the pounds (Luke 19:11–27), and the parable of the talents (Matt. 25:14–30).

2. Metaphorically, believers are the ground which brings forth fruit according to the parable of the sower (Matt. 13:19ff.; Mark 4:15ff.; Luke 8:12ff.). We are also the branches which bear fruit as we abide in the Vine (John 15:5), the grain of wheat which brings forth fruit if it dies (John 12:24), and the trees which are known by their fruit (Matt. 7:19, 20).

3. Both in Ephesians 5:9 and Galatians 5:22 we have the word *karpós*, "fruit," in the singular and not in the plural. It is a quality of life that is spoken of here as being fruitful in contrast to individual good deeds.

   a) Such a mind-set will in turn manifest the fruit of light as enumerated in Ephesians 5:9: "all kinds of goodness [*agathōsúnē*, 'benevolence'] and righteousness [*dikaiosúnē*, 'rendering to God His rights'] and truth [as opposed to lying]."

    *b)* Paul lists additional fruit in Galatians 5:22, 23: love (*agápē*, "unselfishly meeting the needs of others"); joy (*chará*, "rejoicing no matter what the circumstances"; see 2 Cor. 7:4; Col. 1:11, 24; 1 Thess. 1:6; James 1:2; 1 Pet. 4:13); peace (*eirénē*, "tranquility in spite of the opposing forces we experience in the world"); long-suffering (*makrothumía*, "patience toward people"); gentleness (*chrēstótēs*, "benevolence"); faith (*pístis*, "trusting God when circumstances tempt us to give up"); meekness (*praótēs*, "active opposition to evil"); and temperance (*egkráteia*, "self-control").

## III. Being in the Light Involves Constantly Testing Ourselves

A. On the positive side, Paul calls this "Proving what is acceptable unto the Lord" (Eph. 5:10).

    1. The word *dokimázontes* means "testing, putting something to trial, to judge whether it is fit and proper."

    2. As Christians, it is possible to act without proper discretion or what James calls "the wisdom that is from above" (James 3:17). Christ also warned us against "throwing our pearls before swine" (Matt. 7:6).

    3. Our unchanging standard must be "what is acceptable unto the Lord."

B. On the negative side, we are instructed to "Have no fellowship with the unfruitful works of darkness, but rather reprove them" (Eph. 5:11).

    1. The children of darkness sometimes have works more vigorous and persistent than the children of light, but their works will not last.

*a*) What are the poisonous products of darkness? The works of the flesh are listed in Galatians 5:19–21, "adultery, fornication, uncleanness [spiritually], lasciviousness [*asélgeia*, 'readiness for as much pleasure as possible'], idolatry ['elevating anybody or anything to the status of deity'], witchcraft [which includes drug addiction], hatred, variance [quarrelings], emulations [jealousies], wrath [outbursts of passionate anger], strife [party factions arising from selfish ambition], seditions [dissentions and discords], heresies [introduction of false beliefs], envyings [desiring evil upon others], murders, drunkenness, revelings [feasting and carousing]."

*b*) Paul also lists similar deeds of darkness in Colossians 3:5–9. A Christian cannot participate in any of these things without adversely affecting the light of his witness.

2. The Bible assures us that the fruits of darkness will be destroyed.

*a*) Paul expresses this in Romans 6:21, "What fruit had ye then in those things whereof ye are now ashamed? for the end of those things is death."

*b*) In Romans 7:5 he describes the unregenerate life as producing fruit "unto death."

*c*) When Paul speaks of the works of darkness as being unfruitful, he means that they cannot feed the soul or spirit of man. They simply satisfy the senses and will quickly fade away. Only what is done for Christ will last forever and ever (1 Cor. 3:11–15):

3. The very nature of a genuine Christian as light will expose and judge the works of darkness (John 3:20; Eph. 5:13).

4. To have fellowship with, to share in what is useless and temporary is to deny the eternal life we have in Christ.

C. The proper exercise of this testing will make us true "followers of God, as dear children" (Eph. 5:1).

# Free to Think as You Should

Key Verse: Philippians 2:5

---

I. **Our Thoughts Show What We Are**
   A. "Action-readers"
      1. If we could read the minds of others, we would know how to best deal with them. Since we do not have that ability, we can only know what they think by how they externalize their thoughts in words and action.
      2. Life becomes torturous to a person who acts contrary to his beliefs. James calls such a one "unstable" and likens him to "a wave of the sea" (James 1:8).
   B. The God-controlled mind
      1. When a sinner believes in Christ, the heart is not only purified, but something happens to his thought process as well. It is changed. He ceases to be a free-thinker and begins to think like Christ.
      2. In 2 Timothy 1:7 Paul tells us what kind of a mind God gives to a saved person: "For God hath not given us the spirit [thought process] of fear [timidity, cowardice], but of power, and of love, and of a sound mind [*sōphronismós*, 'a disciplined mind']."
         *a*) Paul informs the Philippians that this is not a passive process however: "Let this mind be in you, which was also in Christ Jesus" (Phil. 2:5).
         *b*) The Greek verb *phroneístho* is in the present imperative voice, which indicates that we are commanded to continually have the mind of Christ.

89

3. We can determine who or what is controlling our thoughts. The greatest possession in life is not money or other worldly goods, but the freedom to think as we please.

## II. It Is Our Duty to Practice the Humility Demonstrated by Christ

A. Although Jesus had always been in the form of God (John 10:30; Phil. 2:6), He gave up this glory to accomplish the purpose of His incarnation (Phil. 2:7).

B. He purposely chose a degrading death for our sakes (Phil. 2:8).

C. Because He thus subjected Himself, God the Father exalted Him (Phil. 2:9).

D. His future rule was assured because of His present obedience (Phil. 2:8, 9).

# The Ultimate in Expectations

Key Verse: Philippians 3:8

---

I. **To What Are You Looking Forward?**
   A. Is it material possessions? They will perish, for you cannot take them with you when you die.
   B. Is it relationships? Separation is inevitable.
   C. Is it fame and achievement? They will not truly satisfy.

II. **Paul Had a Different Expectation**
   A. His goal was to obtain "the excellency of the knowledge of Christ Jesus my Lord" (Phil. 3:8). The participial noun for excellency (*tó huperéchon*) means "that which is superior" (also used in Phil. 2:3; 4:7). Paul realized that his ultimate goal was above him and something to reach for (Phil. 3:12). The person who thinks he is already sufficient is miserable, while the blessed person is one who possesses by faith that which is beyond his power or capabilities (Phil. 3:9). What is it that must be attained by faith? It is the knowledge (*gnōsis*, "experiential knowledge") of Christ Jesus.
      1. "Christ Jesus" is a post-resurrection appellation of our Lord, indicating that the resurrection proved Him to be superior to all created beings. Indeed He is the very Creator and Sustainer of life itself (John 1:3, 4; Col. 1:17).
      2. Knowing the human Jesus to be Christ, the anointed of God, is the ultimate knowledge. To know Him by

        personally following Him is to possess the ultimate that life can offer.

3. We cannot have a relationship with Christ unless we make Him Master as well as Savior. Observe that Paul says "my Lord" (*Kúrios*, "Master").

B. Paul also desired to "know him, and the power of his resurrection" (Phil. 3:10). The word used for "know" (*gnōnai*) indicates that initial knowledge of Christ as Savior imparts to the believer the same power Jesus demonstrated when He broke loose the bonds of death. It is what Jesus meant by having "everlasting life" (John 3:16).

C. There is, however, a condition to be met. That is: "being made conformable unto his death" (Phil. 3:10). In order to obtain "the resurrection of the dead" which Paul mentions (Phil. 3:11), we must die to ourselves in order to serve God and others.

D. The verb *summorphoúmenos*, "made conformable," is actually in the middle voice in Greek and not the passive. We are active in achieving our ultimate goal as Christians by putting Christ's will above our own in our daily lives.

# Guidelines for the Christian Life

Key Verse: Philippians 4:8

---

I. **The Christians in Philippi Came Out of a Heathen Environment**
   A. Most of those who lived in Philippi practiced ways of life which were totally unacceptable for a Christian.
   B. Other actions were not bad in themselves, but the motivation behind them was wrong. For instance, in heathendom, stealing may have been avoided because of the severe punishment one would receive if caught. Although the resulting behavior may be the same as that espoused by Christianity, the Christian is motivated by a desire to please Christ, not merely to avoid punishment. In a similar manner, Christians today live in a society which contains many heathen practices. We must be as diligent to avoid evil as the early Philippian Christians were.

II. **The Christian Must Make a Choice Between His Old Lifestyle and the New One in Jesus Christ**
   A. In making our decision we must use our reason (Phil. 4:8). The translators have rendered the present indicative *logízomai* in Philippians 3:13, "Brethren, I count [*logízomai*] not myself to have apprehended." To translate this verb as simply "think" or "let the mind dwell" is inadequate. It really means using one's mind to come to the right conclusion.
   B. The motives of our hearts must also be pure. That element of the Christian's conduct is indicated by the use

of the relative pronoun *hósa*, "whatsoever things," referring to the qualities listed in Philippians 4:8.

C. Christian behavior is not an automatic result of salvation; it is learned by conscious practice and imitation, by conforming to His Word.

1. "Those things, which ye have both learned . . ." (Phil. 4:9). The word for "learned" is *emáthete*. It refers to a lesson not only taught, but more importantly, learned.

2. "Those things, which ye have both learned, and received. . . ." *Parelábete* is the aorist indicative active of *paralambánō*, "to accept" (see 1 Cor. 15:1, 3; Gal. 1:9). The Philippians had made Paul's instructions a part of their own way of life.

3. "Those things, which ye have both learned, and received, and heard, and seen in me. . . ." Paul was not only their teacher but also their example since he practiced what he had preached to them.

4. "Those things . . . do." Actually, the antecedents of the plural demonstrative pronoun *taúta*, "those things," are the things listed in verse eight using the relative pronoun *hósa*, "whatsoever things." The verb "do" is *prássete*, the present imperative of *prássō*, expressing an action as continued or not yet completed. Thus, we are urged to continue behaving as Christians in our daily lives in order to show the world that Christ lives within us (Phil. 1:21).

III. **The Apostle Paul Gives Us General Guidelines on Which to Base Our Actions**

A. ". . . Whatsoever things are true . . ." (Phil. 4:8). The word for "true" is *alēthḗ*, meaning "sincere, genuine, and not fake" (see 1 Cor. 5:8; Phil. 1:18). When our thoughts are centered upon things that are genuine, our actions will not be hypocritical.

B. ". . . Whatsoever things are honest. . . ." The Greek for "honest" is *semná*. This adjective was used of certain Greek gods and goddesses who were considered worthy of reverence and worship. Used here to modify "things" it means "dignified" or "causing respect." *Semná* (plural of *semnós* which is from *sébomai*, "to reverence") first occurs here in Philippians 4:8 and refers to things such as clothing, actions or speech (in 1 Tim. 3:8 it refers to deacons, in 3:11 to women, and in Titus 2:2 to old men). Therefore, whatever we wear, do, or say should command respect.

C. ". . . Whatsoever things are just. . . ." There is man's righteousness (Matt. 4:20) and God's righteousness. It is necessary to search the Scriptures to find out what is right and acceptable to God.

D. ". . . Whatsoever things are pure. . . ." The Greek word here is *hagná*, which means "chaste, freedom from defilements or impurities" (2 Cor. 11:2; 1 Tim. 5:22; Titus 2:5; 1 Pet. 3:2; 1 John 3:3). It could also refer to purity from sexual defilement (2 Cor. 11:2).

E. ". . . Whatsoever things are lovely. . . ." The word *prosphilés* is unique to this passage and is derived from the preposition *prós*, "to," and *phílos*, "friend," or *philéō*, "to love or befriend." The best rendering would be "endearing things." What we think and do then should endear us to God and others.

F. ". . . Whatsoever things are of good report. . . ." The word *eúphēma* is used only here. It is derived from *eu*, "good" and *phémē*, "fame," which is from the verb *phēmí*, "speak or make known." Thus, we should concentrate on things which are well-spoken of.

G. The two items which follow this list in Philippians 4:8 are in the singular: ". . . if there be any virtue, and if there be any praise. . . ." The word for virtue is *areté* (2 Pet. 1:3, 5), derived from the verb *aréskō*, "to please." Aristotle spoke of *areté* as the middle ground between two extremes. How important it is for a Christian to take a balanced view of life according to Scripture. Secondly, the word for "praise" is *épainos* (Phil. 1:11), from *epí*, "upon," and *aínos*, "praise" (Matt. 21:16; Luke 18:43). The compound noun *épainos* means that which deserves praise. Any praiseworthy object in God's eyes is worthy of our consideration.

IV. **The Reward for Living in a Christian Manner Is the Presence of God in Our Lives**

The last phrase of verse nine, ". . . and the God of peace shall be with you" should rather say ". . . then the God. . . ." We shall have not only the peace of God, but also the God from whom peace emanates as our constant companion. A Holy God does not like to keep company with unholy people who unworthily carry the name of His Son, Jesus Christ.

# Do You Have Resurrection Life?

Key Verse: Colossians 3:1

---

I. **Look for the Vital Signs**
   A. Colossians 3:1 does not begin with a supposition but with the vital fact of spiritual life. The NIV correctly translates *ei* as "since," instead of "if": "Since, then, you have been raised with Christ. . . ." This verse describes the new life that is ours when we receive Christ as Lord and accept His sacrifice on our behalf (Rom. 6:3–6; Col. 2:12). Paul states it this way, "I am crucified with Christ: nevertheless I live; yet not I, but Christ liveth in me: and the life which I now live in the flesh I live by the faith of the Son of God, who loved me, and gave himself for me" (Gal. 2:20). Resurrection life is thus lived by faith in Christ.
   B. Another vital sign is the fact that Christ now lives through me. My actions display His will rather than my own.

II. **Resurrection Life Focuses on Things Above**
   A. In Colossians 3:1 the verb for "seek" [*zēteíte*] is in the present imperative, stongly implying a constant seeking. We must constantly put God's kingdom first. One practical application of this principle would be to invest our resources in propagating the gospel rather than spending all our time and money improving our earthly living (Matt. 6:19, 20).
   B. Secondly, Paul tells us to keep our hearts or "affection on things above" (Col. 3:2). The verb *phroneíte*, "set

your affection," is also in the present imperative, implying continuity. The lust of the flesh is striving constantly for the affection of our hearts.

C. Next, we must mortify the flesh, which manifests itself in "fornication, uncleanness, inordinate affection, evil concupiscence, and covetousness, which is idolatry" (Col. 3:5). "Mortify" is not in the present imperative, however, but in the aorist imperative, which means to kill once and for all these tendencies of our old natures. If we fail to do so, we will still be under God's wrath and not His grace (Col. 3:6, 7), no matter what our profession (Matt. 7:21).

D. We must also put away those practices which characterized our previous spiritual deadness, ". . . anger, wrath, malice, blasphemy, filthy communication out of your mouth" (Col. 3:8). Again, the Greek verb *apóthesthe* is in the aorist middle imperative, implying a once and for all rejection of these actions.

E. "Lie not one to another" (Col. 3:9). The Greek verb, *pseúdesthe*, is the present imperative, indicating continuity. To a Christian, this sin might be more tempting as it is less blatant than the others. Its seriousness, nevertheless, is seen in the fact that one whole verse is devoted to it alone.

### III. The Secret of "Put Off" is "Put On"

A. The participle "put on" in verse ten is *endusámenoi* in the aorist active, and implies a once and for all putting on of the new man at our conversion.

B. Our renewed minds will keep our hearts on things above, and earth will lose its attraction.

C. As long as we are in this body, however, it will take constant effort on our part to be renewed in mind (Rom. 12:2).

# How Should a Christian Behave?

Key Verse: Colossians 3:12

I. **Recognize Who You Are (Col. 3:12)**
   A. Being a believer in Jesus Christ means to be chosen (*eklektoí*). What a unique privilege to be chosen out of the whole world to become a child of God!
   B. Paul states that, "as the elect of God," we are both "holy and beloved."
      1. The proof that our faith is genuine is our desire for holy living. Although we will fail from time to time (1 John 1:8), we should be steadily progressing toward a more godly life.
      2. Likewise, we are beloved of God (*ēgapēménoi*) and, therefore, should continue to reflect His love.

II. **Act as a Chosen One (Col. 3:12)**
   A. Paul tells us to clothe ourselves (*endúsasthe*) with several qualities in order to glorify God. Because the verb "clothe" is in the aorist imperative, it indicates this is a definitive act we must engage in after we are saved.
   B. He lists certain inner attitudes which are to be manifested outwardly.
      1. First mentioned are "bowels of compassion." *Splágchna* (translated "bowels") in Greek refers to the inward parts of the body, such as the heart, lungs, and liver which are essential to life itself.
      2. The second attitude Paul instructs us to adopt is that of kindness (*chrēstótēs*) which may also be translated as "goodness" or "gentleness" (Rom. 2:4;

3:12; 11:22; 2 Cor. 6:6; Gal. 5:22; Eph. 2:7; Titus 3:4).

3. Next is humility (*tapeinophrosúnē*), which means to consider ourselves as being lowly. Without this virtue we may begin to consider ourselves spiritually higher than others whom we are assisting.

4. Meekness (*praótēs*) further indicates that we must exercise discernment when approaching any situation, especially in regard to our own importance and the true needs of others.

5. Finally, long-suffering (*makrothumía*) is mentioned by Paul. We must never give up on anybody because if God had given up on us, where would we be (Rom. 2:4; 9:22; 2 Cor. 6:6; 1 Tim. 1:16; 1 Pet. 3:20; 2 Pet. 3:15)?

### III. Uphold Others and Extend Grace to Them (Col. 3:13)

A. The word translated "forbearing" is *anechómenoi* in the Greek and is derived from *aná*, "up," and *échomai*, "to hold." Thus, the philosophy of the Christian is not to "live and let live," but rather "watch who is floundering in order to uphold him."

B. The expression "one another" is derived from *állos*, which means "another of the same kind" (as opposed to *héteros*, "another of a different kind"). In effect, Paul is telling us that we are all going to require support at some period in our lives due to our common human frailty.

C. Likewise, we are also to forgive each other "even as Christ forgave you." Here the verb *charizómenoi* is used rather than *aphíēmi*, "to remove the blame," signifying forgiveness of the debt owed (Luke 7:42, 43; 2 Cor. 2:7, 10; 12:13). In such cases we are to forfeit our rights in order to show the love of Christ both to the members of the body of Christ and to the watching world (John 17:21).

# Why Should We Be Thankful?

Key Verse: 1 Thessalonians 1:2

---

I. **The Apostle Paul Clearly Gives Us an Example of a Thankful Attitude**

A. In nearly every epistle, Paul's first words are those of thanksgiving and praise to God.

  1. Paul made this suggestion in 1 Thessalonians 5:18: "In everything give thanks. . . ."

  2. Paul's thanksgiving was not dependent on his personal circumstances. He continued to thank God despite many hardships (2 Cor. 11:22–33).

  3. Paul's thanksgiving is evidenced in prayer (1 Thess. 1:2).

    *a*) For Paul, this externalizing was spontaneous, flowing out of his love for Christ and the saints of Christ's Church.

    *b*) We should echo Paul, as we recognize our indebtedness to God for the gift of life itself and for His providence in sustaining us (2 Cor. 1:8–11).

B. Paul used the Greek word for thanksgiving often.

  1. The word for thanksgiving in Greek is *eucharistía*, from *eu*, "well," and *cháris*, "grace, thanks." When we consider God's *cháris*, "grace," we are compelled to have *eucharistía*, "thanksgiving."

  2. In pre-Christian Greek literature, however, the word *eucharistía* is rarely used.

  3. Outside the Gospels and Revelation, the word "thanksgiving" occurs in the New Testament only in the writings of Paul.

*a*) The word *eucharistía*, itself does not actually occur in the Gospels, but similar words are used such as *euloēgsas*, "blessed" (Matt. 26:26; Mark 14:22) and *eucharistēsas*, "having given thanks" (Luke 22:17; John 6:11, 23).

*b*) The noun appears only twice in Revelation, which was written long after all of Paul's epistles, so it is quite possible that John borrowed Paul's usage.

## II. For Paul, Thanksgiving Is Also a Duty

A. In 1 Thessalonians 1:2, the KJV says, "We give thanks to God always for you all. . . ."

1. Paul expresses thanksgiving as simply something he does (1 Thess. 1:2). But in 2 Thessalonians 1:3 the Greek text has the expression, *opheílomen eucharisteín*, translated "we are bound to thank," or "it is our duty to thank God always for you."

2. Paul further declares that thanksgiving is not an elective exercise but mandatory (2 Thess. 2:13).

B. In 1 Thessalonians chapters one and two, Paul connects the duty of thanksgiving with prayer, "We give thanks to God always for you all making mention of you in our prayers."

1. We must thank God for others' benefits and blessings as well as for ourselves. In order to do this we must have others on our minds as we go to prayer.

2. If we practice this form of thanksgiving, it will revolutionize our own lives and our relationships with others.

C. Paul elsewhere stresses the necessity of thanksgiving. He attributes the darkness of the heathen world to a lack of thanksgiving and praise (Rom. 1:21).

### III. What Should Be the Extent of Our Thanksgiving? (1 Thess. 1:2)

A. Paul tells us our thanksgiving should be "always."

    1. Thanksgiving and prayers must be constant attitudes manifested all day long, seven days a week. Note how many times the word, *pántote*, "always," occurs in this connection (Rom. 1:9; 1 Cor. 1:4; Eph. 5:20; Col. 1:3; 4:12; 1 Thess. 3:6; 2 Thess. 1:3, 11; 2:13; Phile. 1:4).

    2. This does not mean we are constantly praying, but that we are always ready to pray and alert for opportunities to pray (Col. 4:2).

B. Paul also stresses that our thanksgiving should be inclusive, "for you all."

    1. Paul did not leave anyone out in verse two, "for you all." Every believer that is a part of a local congregation has been called into the body of Christ.

    2. Therefore every member is vitally important to every other member of the church. In each member of our church we can find reason for praise on the fact of his calling alone. Yet above this, we ought to seek to be able as well to give God praise for the spiritual qualities we see in each one.

C. Paul further instructs us that our thanksgiving should be informed.

    1. A believer must exercise his memory as he gives thanks in prayer.

        *a)* In 1 Thessalonians 1:2 Paul says, ". . . making mention of you . . . ," or, in other words, recalling each believer by name. The word *mneía*, "remembrance or mention," is always used in connection with prayer (Rom. 1:9; Eph. 1:16; 1 Thess. 1:2; Phile. 1:4).

*b*) In order to bring others before God in prayer, we must first be able to *mnēmoneúontes*, "to call to mind." This verb form is followed by the adverb *adialeíptōs*, "without ceasing, without allowing any lapse of time" (Rom. 1:9; 2 Thess. 2:13). Thus we must constantly be filling our memory bank with the names and faces of fellow believers as did Paul.

2. A believer must also exercise his observation to feed his memory.

   *a*) We should detect how faith manifests itself in what others do, and find things in their lives worth imitating.

      (1) Some may be weary from doing their work for Christ's kingdom. The word for labor in 1 Thessalonians 1:3 is *kópos*, "fatigue resulting from labor." We should likewise be diligent.

      (2) Others may be carrying heavy burdens of life. The word for "patience" is *hupomonē*. It implies being hopeful despite the circumstances. Seeing such patience causes our faith to increase as well.

   *b*) We must likewise remember all these needs of our brothers and sisters in Christ as we offer up prayers for them continually, thanking God especially for their faith and inclusion in the eternal life to come.

# Paul's Model of an Effective Ministry

Key Verse: 1 Thessalonians 2:4

I. Luke Describes Paul's Brief Ministry in Thessalonica
   (Acts 17:1–9)
   A. As was his custom, Paul first went to the synagogue
      where it was natural to find God-fearing people (Acts
      17:1, 2).
   B. He then presented the gospel to them in an intelligent
      manner, ". . . reasoned with them out of the Scrip-
      tures" (Acts 17:2).
      1. The verb "reasoned" is *dielégeto*, the imperfect of
         *dialégomai*, which is derived from *diá*, "through,"
         and *légō*, "to speak intelligently." It is the word from
         which "dialectic" comes, that branch of logic which
         teaches the art of logically discerning the truth.
      2. This method of preaching was used by Paul in
         Athens (Acts 17:17), in Corinth (Acts 18:4), in
         Ephesus (Acts 18:19; 19:8), in Troas (Acts 20:7, 9),
         and before Felix (Acts 24:25).
   C. His messages were "out of the Scriptures" (Acts 17:2)
      and presented "the gospel of God" (1 Thess. 2:2).
      1. This gospel included the necessary death and resur-
         rection of Christ (Acts 17:3).
      2. He identified Jesus as the anointed of God in spite
         of the fact that he knew it would cause the Jews to
         hate him (Acts 17:5).
   D. Paul taught at the synagogue for only three Sabbaths.
      Here is a church established as a result of preaching
      three times.

1. What a joy it must have been for Paul to say to the Thessalonians, "For yourselves, brethren, know our entrance in unto you, that it was not in vain" (1 Thess. 2:1). The word for "in vain" is *kenē*, "empty, accomplished nothing." Preaching must accomplish something; otherwise it is empty.
2. Paul's ministry was effective in that those to whom he preached "believed" (1 Thess. 2:10).
3. Not all believed, but some did (Acts 17:4).
4. Those who believed remained faithful under pressure.

E. Disturbance and persecution arose, but the church of the Thessalonians was firmly established.
   1. Paul's concern for the faithfulness of this infant church proved to be unfounded (1 Thess. 3:5, 6).
   2. Paul's ministry, although short and turbulent, was successful.

## II. In His Letter, Paul Pinpoints the Effective Characteristics of His Ministry in Thessalonica

A. Paul spoke very boldly, ". . . we were bold in our God to speak unto you the gospel of God . . ." (1 Thess. 2:2).
   1. The Greek verb is *parrēsiázomai*, "to speak boldly, to be free, frank, bold in speech, demeanor, or action." It is characteristic of Paul's preaching (Acts 9:27, 29; 13:46; 14:3; 18:26; 19:8; Eph. 6:20).
   2. This boldness took real effort on Paul's part. In verse two the Greek word *agōn* translated "contention" (KJV) should be rendered "with great struggle."
      *a*) Paul faced conflict internally as well as externally when he spoke out boldly for Christ.
      *b*) His boldness, then, was not simply free speech, but speaking the gospel freely even in the face of opposition (Acts 17:5).

B. Paul taught the truth (1 Thess. 2:3). The word "exhortation" is *paráklēsis*, literally meaning "a calling near" as in Acts 13:15 and 15:31.

   1. Some teaching of the word of God according to Paul, can be "of deceit" instead of bringing us nearer to God.

   2. In verse three he also mentions teaching "of uncleanness," referring to teaching that justifies moral sin. *Akatharsía*, "uncleanness," refers to lewdness as opposed to chastity (Rom. 1:24; 6:19; 2 Cor. 12:21; Gal. 5:19; Eph. 4:19; 5:3; Col. 3:5; 1 Thess. 4:7). We should also examine the lifestyle of the preacher, as well as his instruction, on the subject of purity (1 Tim. 3:2; Titus 1:6) before giving him credence.

   3. Teaching can also be done in a fraudulent way, *en dólō*, "in guile."

      *a*) The preposition used here is *en*, "in," or by means of, and the noun is *dólos* derived from *délear*, "bait."

      *b*) False teachers will bait us with watered down truths in order to attract us to their own incorrect teaching.

      *c*) With our Lord, on the other hand, there was never *dólos*, "guile," in His mouth (1 Pet. 2:22).

C. Paul indicates that he was not a man-pleaser: ". . . not as pleasing men, but God . . ." (1 Thess. 2:4).

D. Neither did he use flattery, "For neither at any time used we flattering words . . ." (1 Thess. 2:5).

E. Paul had no selfish motives for his teaching ". . . nor a cloak of covetousness" (1 Thess. 2:5). What is translated "a cloak" is *próphasis*, "a pretext, an excuse."

   1. Paul did not seek financial rewards as his reason for ministry. A Bible teacher should not find pretexts for acquiring material wealth from the people to whom he ministers.

2. Paul also did not seek glory or recognition from men (1 Thess. 2:6).

3. Far from being a burden (1 Thess. 2:6), Paul actually supported himself during his ministry.

    *a*) He did not demand more than his rights or even ask to be given his legitimate right, so that the gospel would not be hindered (1 Cor. 9:11, 12; 2 Thess. 3:7–9).

    *b*) One wonders how much the gospel is being hindered today by those who are unwilling to follow Paul's example.

F. Paul was *hḗpios*, "gentle" in 1 Thessalonians 2:7, as opposed to being a fighter, described in 2 Timothy 2:24, "And the servant of the Lord must not strive [*máchesthai*, 'to fight as if in war or in battle']."

1. He describes his gentleness in this way:

    *a*) He was "as a nurse" (v. 7), which conveys the idea of providing food—here the food was the word of God.

    *b*) He also said that he was as a nurse who "cherisheth her children" (v. 7). This word figuratively means "to brood."

2. Paul's gentleness went beyond just giving a message. Paul was ready to communicate not only the gospel, but also himself (1 Thess. 3:8). It was all these aspects of his teaching that made his ministry among the Thessalonians so successful.

# What Kind of Joy Do You Want?

Key Verse: 1 Thessalonians 5:16

I. **Joy Is a Distinctive Characteristic of the Christian Life**
   A. In Greek the verb for "rejoice" is *chaírō* (Phil. 3:1; 4:4; Col. 1:24; 1 Thess. 3:9; 5:16) and the noun is *chará*, "joy" (John 15:11; 16:20; Col. 1:11; 1 Thess. 1:6; 3:9).
      1. Both words are related to *cháris*, "grace." The permanence of joy as a quality of life is only possible as a result of the appropriation of the grace of God through faith in Jesus Christ.
      2. A Christian who can say, "But by the grace of God I am what I am" has appropriated that source of joy (1 Cor. 15:10).
   B. This kind of joy (*chará*) is very closely connected with other Christian virtues.
      1. In Romans 14:17, it is linked with righteousness and peace.
      2. The Bible also ranks "joy" second in a list of the fruit of the Spirit (Gal. 5:22), the first being "love."
      3. References to joy in the Christian life are frequent (Acts 2:46; 8:39; 13:52; 16:34; Rom. 12:12; 2 Cor. 1:24; 8:2; Phil. 1:25; 1 Pet. 1:8).
   C. Joy is portrayed in the Bible not as a static state but as a state of growth in which the Christian willfully cooperates with God (2 Cor. 13:11; Phil. 3:1; 4:4; 1 Thess. 5:16; James 1:2; 1 Pet. 4:13).
      1. Paul even makes the attainment of joy an object of prayer (Rom. 15:13).

2. Paul also represents the achievement of joy as one of the goals of his apostolic ministry to the churches (2 Cor. 1:24; Phil. 1:25).

D. Paul also instructs us that this state of rejoicing is to be constant. "Rejoice evermore" (1 Thess. 5:16) is the admonition of Scripture.

  1. The word for rejoice is *chaírete*, a verb meaning "be joyful."

     *a*) It is in the present tense, imperative mood, which involves continuity, and not that sporadic rejoicing which emanates from a mere satisfying experience.

     *b*) To the contrary, we are instructed to have a permanent frame of mind that rejoices without regard to our circumstances. The word *pántote*, translated as "evermore," could be better rendered as "always" (NASB, NIV), meaning, "at all times, no matter what the circumstances are."

  2. The New Testament teaches that the Christian life involves the creation of a new personality. There is a new kind of existence which makes a permanent change in the person (2 Cor. 5:17).

     *a*) A Christian is a new person whose source of joy is internal, "which is Christ in you, the hope of glory" (Col. 1:27).

     *b*) *Makárioi*, "blessed" (Matt. 5:1–12; Luke 6:20–23), are those indwelt by God for the sake of Jesus Christ (Matt. 5:11; Luke 6:22) and who, because of that indwelling, find their full joy or satisfaction (John 15:11).

## II. There Is a Different Concept of Joy in the World

A. In Greek, "hedonism" (*hēdonē*), denotes joy in the sensual realm (Luke 8:14; Titus 3:3; James 4:1, 3; 2 Pet. 2:13). *Hēdonē*, "sensual pleasure," is the source of joy in this worldly philosophy.

B. Another type of joy is described as "being merry" (*euphraínō*, Luke 12:19; 15:23, 24, 29, 32; 16:19; Acts 2:26; 7:41; 14:17; Rom. 15:10; 2 Cor. 2:2; Gal. 4:27; Rev. 11:10; 12:12). This word comes the closest of any in the New Testament in its meaning to the English word "happy."

   1. The two Greek words which could most accurately be translated "happy," *eutuchḗs*, "one with good luck," or *eudaímōn*, "fortunate, happy because of favor shown," do not occur in the New Testament at all.

   2. Whenever the word "happy" is used in any translation of the New Testament, it really should be translated "blessed." It is a translation from the Greek word *makários* (John 13:17; Acts 26:2; Rom. 14:22; 1 Cor. 7:40; James 5:11; 1 Pet. 3:14; 4:14).

C. "Being of good cheer" (*euthuméō*) is another state of mind described in Acts 27:22, 25 and James 5:13. The adjective *eúthumos* is also found in Acts 27:36 and the adverb *euthúmōs* in Acts 24:10.

   1. These words denote hopeful good cheer and often refer to the outcome of a certain situation or undertaking. Such a feeling is by definition temporary in its nature.

   2. This demonstration of cheer can be experienced by both the Christian and non-Christian alike.

## III. The Scriptures Reveal Other Spiritual Pleasures Which Are Enduring in Contrast to the Fluctuating Joys of the World

A. There are several other terms used to describe these spiritual joys.

   1. The Greek word *agallíasis* means "exultation" (Luke 1:14, 44; Acts 2:46; Heb. 1:9; Jude 1:24) and the verb *agalliáō*, "to exult" (Matt. 5:12; Luke 1:47; 10:21; John 5:35; 8:56; Acts 2:26; 16:34; 1 Pet. 1:6,

8; 4:13; Rev. 19:7). Worship and praise cause the believer to experience spiritual joy.

2. Another related term is *kaucháomai*, "boast," in which state we appreciate our exulted position (Rom. 2:17, 23; 5:2, 3, 11; 1 Cor. 1:29, 31; 3:21; 4:7; 2 Cor. 5:12; 7:14; 9:2; 10:8, 13, 15, 17; 11:12, 16, 18, 30; 12:1, 5, 6, 9; Gal. 6:13, 14; Eph. 2:9; Phil. 3:3; James 1:9; 4:16). As can be seen by these references, it is possible to have the wrong object as the focus of our boasting or exulting, in which case our joy will not be lasting.

B. The Scriptures also reveal the kinds of conditions which lead to spiritual rejoicing.

1. The consciousness of our salvation (Rom. 5:11; Phil. 3:8; 4:1–10) is a source of our joy, as are also faith, hope, and truth (Acts 8:39; 16:34; Rom. 15:3; 1 Cor. 13:6; 2 Cor. 1:24; Phil. 1:25; 1 Pet. 1:8).

2. Being filled with the Spirit is also equated with being filled with joy (Acts 2:46; 13:52; Rom. 14:17).

3. The anticipation of the life to come in heaven fills the believer with joy (Rom. 14:17; 15:13; Heb. 10:34; 1 Pet. 1:6, 8; 4:13; Jude 1:24; Rev. 19:7).

4. Lastly, there is an added joy which belongs to the servant of God engaged in the work of God's calling (Acts 20:24; Rom. 16:19; 2 Cor. 6:10; 7:4; Phil. 1:4, 5; 2:2, 17; Col. 1:24; 1 Thess. 3:9), especially as he will see the results of his work when he stands before God (2 Cor. 1:14; Phil. 4:1; 1 Thess. 2:19).

# How to Face Tribulation

Key Verse: 2 Thessalonians 1:7

I. **Persecution, Tribulation, and the Great Tribulation**
   A. Persecution and tribulation are inevitable for unbelievers and believers.
      1. Tribulation is part of the suffering inherent in humanity because of man's disobedience and the Fall.
         *a*) When a person becomes a believer, he does not cease to be part of the human race.
         *b*) All humans, and indeed all creation, groan in vanity (Gen. 2:17; 3:17; John 15:20; 16:33; Acts 14:22; Rom. 5:3; 8:35; 12:12; 2 Cor. 1:4; 7:4; Eph. 3:13; 2 Thess. 1:4; Rev. 1:9; 2:9, 10).
      2. For believers, tribulation is much more tolerable because no matter what happens, Christ makes them victorious and actually causes them to benefit from all circumstances (Heb. 2:6–8). Christ promised peace for us while we are suffering tribulation (John 16:33; Rom. 8:37; 2 Cor. 11:19–33).
   B. A special period of tribulation is coming such as the world has never known.
      1. Jesus discussed it in the Olivet Discourse (Matt. 24:21, 29; Mark 13:19, 24).
         *a*) This is not the ordinary tribulation we all experience now. It is future.
         *b*) It is characterized as "great," thus categorizing all other tribulations as small compared to it (Matt. 24:21).
         *c*) It is going to be a tribulation "such as was not since the beginning of the world to this time,

113

no, nor ever shall be" (Matt. 24:21; Mark 13:19).

2. The detailed description of this period of tribulation is given in Revelation chapters four through nineteen. A simple reading of these chapters and a recollection of history are enough to conclude that the events described have not yet occurred.

3. The period of this tribulation is to be immediately followed by heavenly signs such as the darkening of the sun, the moon not giving her borrowed light (*phéggos*), the stars falling from heaven, and the shaking of the powers of heaven (Matt. 24:29; Mark 13:24; Luke 21:25).

4. The only thing that could possibly connect this period of tribulation with the past, namely the destruction of Jerusalem, would be the reference of our Lord to "the abomination of desolation."

   *a)* If this happened in A.D. 70 when Jerusalem and the temple were destroyed under Titus (Matt. 24:15; Mark 13:14, cf. Luke 21:20), there could be a connection.

   *b)* But since that tribulation did not include the heavenly signs in the sun, the moon, and the stars, and the Son of Man did not come (Matt. 24:29, 30; Mark 13:24–26; Luke 21:25–27), this "abomination of desolation" must be future (Dan. 7:7, 8, 19–27; 9:24–27; 11:36–45; 12:1).

## II. The Thessalonian Believers and Tribulation

A. The Thessalonians were experiencing tribulation in their present state.

1. Paul refers to their tribulation in 2 Thessalonians 1:4 and exulted in their behalf because their patience and faith were holding up.

2. Their participation in the kingdom of God would be proportionate to their endurance and faith in

tribulations and trials (2 Thess. 1:5). God's justice demanded that.

B. It was also part of God's justice "to recompense tribulation to them that troubled" them (2 Thess. 1:6).

  1. The verb "recompense" is the aorist infinitive active of *antapodoúnai*, "to repay, avenge." This means that the recompense is viewed as a specific action, not a process, although the time of occurrence is undefined.

  2. This undoubtedly will be in connection with the tribulation period (Rev. 4—19), or the Day of the Lord (Rev. 20:11–15), the times of judgment for unbelievers.

C. What will the situation of the afflicted believers be?

  1. Will they be further punished by God by being allowed to go through the Tribulation?

    *a)* This would be contrary to logic in view of God's justice.

    *b)* How could it be said that God was punishing those who were afflicting the believers if He allows them to go through the same tribulation?

  2. Paul describes a different expectation for believers. In verse seven Paul tells us what God is going to do for the afflicted believers.

    *a)* "And to you who are troubled [*thliboménois*, 'afflicted,' from the word *thlípsis*, 'tribulation'] rest with us."

      (1) The word for rest is *ánesis* from the verb *aníēmi*, derived from *aná*, "back," or *ánō*, "up," and *híēmi*, "to send," meaning "to send up, let go." Thus *ánesis* here refers to the sending up or letting go of the believers when the Lord shall descend from heaven.

      (2) Their rest is not going to be in Christ as it is during this dispensation, but they will be taken up to be with Christ as explained in

1 Thessalonians 4:13–18. The Thessalonian believers are told to find their comfort in this forthcoming event.

(3) It would not be much comfort and rest if they were to go through the same tribulation as the unbelievers who were afflicting them.

(4) Paul expected to be with them: "And to you who are troubled, rest with us" (2 Thess. 1:7).

b) This is to take place "when the Lord Jesus shall be revealed from heaven." This is when He will come for His saints, an event already described in 1 Thessalonians 4:16.

(1) In 2 Thessalonians 1:7 this event is called the *ánesis*, "letting go up for rest," and the *apokálupsis*, "revelation." In 1 Thessaonians 4:15, however, it is called *parousía*, "coming presence." He will come with His mighty angels (1 Thess 4:16, with the voice of His angels and archangel; 2 Thess. 1:7).

(2) The afflicted believers are going to have the glorious experience of being taken up for rest.

D. What will the situation of the unbelievers be?

1. The unbelievers who persecuted the believers will experience what is described in 2 Thessalonians 1:8: "In flaming fire taking vengeance on them that know not God, and that obey not the gospel of our Lord Jesus Christ."

a) This is the Day of the Lord, the day of judgment for unbelievers (Is. 2:12; 13:6, 9; Ezek. 13:5; 30:3; Joel 1:15; 2:1, 11, 31; 3:14; Amos 5:18, 20; Obad. 1:15; Zeph. 1:7, 14; Zech. 14:1; Mal. 4:5; Acts 2:20; 1 Thess. 5:2; 2 Pet. 3:10).

*b*) This is the day when the Lord Jesus will be "revealed from heaven."

2. In 2 Thessalonians 1:9 Paul explains that the unbelievers shall be punished with everlasting destruction (not extinction, but causing to cease to be what one is, or to be lost) from the presence of the Lord, and from the glory of His power.

E. How does Paul emphasize the distinction?

1. In verse ten Paul reverts to what the Lord will do for His own, which is a far cry from allowing them to go through the Tribulation: "When he shall come to be glorified in His saints, and to be admired in all them that believe (because our testimony among you was believed) in that day."

2. For believers, the Day of The Lord starts simultaneously with the coming of the Lord to take them up; it is the Day of the Lord Jesus or the Day of Christ (1 Cor. 5:5; 2 Cor. 1:14; Phil. 1:6, 10; 2:16).

3. For one who knows the Lord Jesus, that day will be the end of all tribulation. Its glowing promise remains the infinite resource to draw upon while enduring tribulations today and tomorrow in the Christian life.

# God's Righteous Judgment on the Enemies Of the Gospel

## Key Verse: 2 Thessalonians 1:8

---

I. **Believers Need to Know That God Is Going to Exercise Justice Toward Their Oppressors**
  A. God's dealing with Israel's enemies in regard to their rejection of Him morally and spiritually.
    1. The Law of Moses became the standard for God's people.
    2. Israel's enemies were judged according to their disobedience of God's laws.
  B. Paul's instructions to the Thessalonians.
    1. The Thessalonian believers were being persecuted and greatly afflicted (2 Thess. 1:4). Paul's message, therefore, encouraged them to remain faithful to Christ under such severe circumstances.
    2. In addition, as true believers exercising patience and endurance (2 Thess. 1:4), they understood that they were not to take justice into their own hands (Heb. 10:30).
    3. Thirdly, they needed to be assured that no enemy of the gospel could deprive them of the privilege of entrance into the kingdom of God (2 Thess. 1:5). The saddest effect that persecution can have upon a believer is to make him doubt his own salvation. To the contrary, we are to expect trials and opposition (2 Tim. 3:12, 13), not easy sailing.

4. Finally, Paul prays that their suffering will not be a result of their own foolish behavior (2 Thess. 1:5, 11).

## II. God Promises Rewards

A. The reward of believers and the punishment of unbelievers will occur at the revelation of our Lord Jesus from heaven.

B. Furthermore, in 2 Thessalonians 1:7 the word *ánesis*, translated "rest," actually means an uptaking which occurs as a result of the believers being loosened from the grip of the enemy on earth. Thus, they will be freed, while the unbelievers are eternally destroyed (2 Thess. 1:8).

## III. Just as Believers Are Rewarded, Unbelievers Will Be Correspondingly Judged

A. Paul instructs us that believers will definitely be rewarded in heaven for their sacrificial service to Christ (1 Cor. 3:13–15; 2 Cor. 5:10; 2 Tim. 4:8).

B. Likewise, the enemies of Christ will also suffer in hell according to their degree of unbelief and wickedness in this life (2 Thess. 1:6). Thus, God's righteous judgment is fulfilled (Rom. 2:5).

# God Does Not Choose Without Sanctifying

Key Verse: 2 Thessalonians 2:13

---

I. **God's Choice of Believers Is in Accordance to His Foreknowledge**

   A. Paul states it in Romans 8:29, "For whom he did foreknow, he also did predestinate to be conformed to the image of his Son, that he might be the firstborn among many brethren." The human mind cannot fathom the mystery of God's foreknowledge (Is. 55:8, 9).

   B. In Scripture we find that God does exercise His right to choose. However, it is not unto eternal damnation but unto salvation, "Moreover, whom he did predestinate, them he also called: and whom he called, them he also justified: and whom he justified, them he also glorified" (Rom. 8:30).

   C. Furthermore, God's choice does not depend upon nor follow man's expression of faith, ". . . God hath from the beginning chosen you to salvation. . ." (2 Thess. 2:13). The Greek verb translated "hath . . . chosen" is *heíleto*, the second aorist indicative middle of *hairéō*, to choose." This tense indicates that He chose for Himself on His own without any dependence upon man's action or faith. It is the will of God which mysteriously implants faith in the heart of man.

II. **God's Sovereignty Does Not Absolve Man from His Responsibility in Regard to the Gospel**

   A. We as human beings do not know who is predestined to believe and who is not. Therefore, the command of

Christ to all believers is "preach the gospel to every creature" (Mark 16:15).

B. Those who fail to respond, however, cannot blame God for their lack of faith. In Romans 9:22, Paul uses the verb *katērtisména*, "fitted," in the middle voice, thereby denoting that "the vessels of wrath" fitted themselves for destruction.

C. Conversely, verse twenty-three, in referring to "the vessels of mercy," uses the verb "afore prepared" in the active voice (*proētoímasen*) to show that it is God who prepares them for glory and not they themselves.

D. Believers are commanded to "stand fast, and hold the traditions which ye have been taught" (2 Thess. 2:15), and "preach the gospel" (Mark 16:15).

## III. God Does Not Give Salvation Without Sanctification

A. The two words, salvation (*sōtēría*) and sanctification (*hagiasmós*), both occur in 2 Thessalonians 2:13. The preposition *eis* that precedes the Greek word translated "salvation" means "unto" or "for" the purpose of salvation, while the preposition *en* preceding the word translated "sanctification" means "in." Thus, we see that salvation is achieved only in conjunction with sanctification and involves "belief of the truth."

B. Those who confess faith but bear no fruit were never saved in the first place (Matt. 7:21).

## IV. All Three Persons of the Trinity Are Involved in Salvation and Sanctification

A. It is God who chooses "from the beginning."

B. This phrase also recalls the Second Person of the Godhead (John 1:1) toward whose glory we are headed (2 Thess. 2:14).

C. The role of the Holy Spirit is demonstrated in verse thirteen: "through [or 'in'] sanctification of the Spirit."

# Why Jesus Christ Came into the World

Key Verse: 1 Timothy 1:15

---

### I. Paul's Affirmation of Christ's Coming into the World

A. This expression *pistós ho lógos*, "trustworthy the word," occurs only in the pastoral epistles (1 Tim. 1:15; 3:1; 4:9; 2 Tim. 2:11; Titus 3:8).

  1. The expression translated, "A faithful saying," probably referred to statements currently being used in the churches.

  2. Paul is not accepting everything the early church taught. Under the guidance of the Holy Spirit, Paul selected only five expressions as absolutely true, and worthy of being included in Scripture as "faithful." The expression in this verse has two key elements.

B. This word or saying is trustworthy (*pistós*). You may place your faith upon it and you will not be disappointed.

  1. When Christ became flesh (John 1:1, 14), it was God who was taking upon Himself human flesh. He became the one in whom "dwelleth all the fullness of the Godhead bodily" (Col. 2:9). He revealed to men the nature and purpose of God. What He revealed is trustworthy because Christ Himself proved trustworthy.

  2. The dependability and trustworthiness of what one says depends on what he is.

3. What Jesus Christ revealed about God the Father is trustworthy because He proved to be trustworthy in Himself.

C. It is significant that the word *lógos* is used in the expression *pistós ho lógos* which appears several times in the Pastoral Epistles.

1. The Holy Spirit could have led Paul to choose a word such as *rhéma* or *laliá*, "the utterance of God"; or *prophēteía*, "prophecy, the telling forth." These words would merely convey that which God spoke.

2. *Ho lógos* conveys, however, not only what God spoke, but what God became in the incarnation of Jesus Christ. *Lógos* means not only utterance but the intelligence from which the word begins as expression.

   *a*) It is not simply a saying but a fact that Christ came into the world.

   *b*) In John 1:1, He is called *ho lógos* which means "the intelligence that gave birth to the word and the expression of that intelligence."

## II. The Nature of Christ's Coming into the World

A. The means of Christ's coming into the world

1. His coming into the world was not due merely to the physical activity of one man and one woman, as is the case with all created human beings.

   *a*) Christ came, and had to come, through the virgin Mary and divine action (Matt. 1:16, 20, 21; Luke 1:26–35).

   *b*) John 1:14 is sometimes wrongly used to deny this.

   (1) A better translation of John 1:14 would be "became," rather than "was made." The verb

*egéneto* is not passive, but is from the deponent verb *gínomai.*

(2) The *Lógos,* the eternal Word became, by His own volition and through His own power, something He was not before—flesh, having then a human nature as well as the divine nature.

2. Jesus Christ did not become a mere man.

    *a)* He became the representation of humanity while continuing to be what He always was—God. This is why when He spoke of coming into the world, He did not speak of just being born into the world of the virgin Mary, but also of voluntarily coming into the world on His own (John 10:10; 12:46; 16:28).

    *b)* Jesus' answer to Pilate, expressing His sovereignty, put His coming into the world into proper perspective.

        (1) With the words, "To this end was I born [*gegénnēmai,* the first person singular perfect indicative passive of *gennáō,* 'to give birth']," Jesus indicates the time that He came into the world as a human being, and that He was fully man at the time He spoke to Pilate.

        (2) He also said, "and for this cause came I [*elélutha,* first person singular perfect of *érchomai,* 'to come,' which indicates that there was a certain time that He voluntarily came into the world as God of His own accord] into the world, that I should bear witness unto the truth. Everyone that is of the truth heareth my voice" (John 18:37).

    *c)* No other human being could say that He was born into the world but that He also voluntarily came into the world. While He was here on earth, He was not only Man, He was God, or in other words the God-Man. This is the reason His words are trustworthy and the work He came to do, to save sinners, can be depended upon as effective.

B. The personal results of Christ's coming into the world

1. Jesus Christ, in His incarnation as the God-Man, claimed to be equal with God: "As the Father knoweth me, even so know I the Father . . ." (John 10:15); "I and my Father are one" (in essence, Deity; John 10:30); ". . . the Father [is] in me and I in Him" (John 10:38).

   a) Note John 14:11, "Believe me that I am in the Father, and the Father in me. . . ." The verb "am" is not in the Greek text, which indicates that this statement has no chronological limitation. There was never an abdication of deity by Jesus Christ. "At that day ye shall know that I am in my Father, and ye in me, and I in you" (John 14:20), again the verb "am" is not in the Greek text indicating eternal relationship never given up by Jesus Christ.

   b) When He was dying on the cross, He was dying as the God-Man. However, only His humanity, as bearing our sin and its consequence of death, could actually die; hence His cry, "My God, My God, why hast thou forsaken me?" (Matt. 27:46).

2. Yet Jesus also admitted His Father's superiority, either in being or in knowledge, as in John 14:28, ". . . for my Father is greater than I."

   a) Notice that the verb *estí*, "is," is used in the Greek text to indicate that the chronological limitation only relates to the Christ's human nature. Jesus Christ was speaking of Himself as Man only—stressing His humiliation (Phil. 2:6–8).

b) In Matthew 24:36 we find, "But of that day and hour knoweth no man, no, not the angels of heaven but my Father only." See also Mark 13:32.

   (1) If He as God-Incarnate did not know, how could He say that only the Father knew? Since He was saying "No man knoweth [*oudeís*, 'no one or no created being' as in John 1:18]," He was referring to Himself as merely man—as brought into the world by the virgin Mary.

   (2) Mere men do not know, but the Son of God knows. Otherwise He must cease to be omniscient, being ignorant of something. Likewise, if the Father knows something that the Son does not, then there must either be a division in the essence of God's being, or the Son must cease to be God. The revelation of the time of His Second Coming was not a part of what He came to make known in His appearance as the God-Man.

## III. The Purpose of Christ's Coming into the World

A. The purpose of the incarnation is stated quite clearly in 1 Timothy 1:15, "that Christ Jesus came [*élthen*, he came voluntarily as the God-Man, not merely being born into the world] into the world to save sinners."

  1. He came into the world, He became flesh, because the blood is in the flesh. He had to have blood to shed because without the shedding of blood there could be no remission of sins (Heb. 9:22).

2. With the shedding of His blood He accomplished:

   *a*) The satisfaction of God's justice in fulfilling the eternal pronouncement that "the wages of sin is death" (Rom. 6:23). This is the reason why Jesus Christ, as the God-Man, had to die in order to remove sin from man (Rom. 5:12–21). The sin of man could not be expiated, blotted out, without the shedding of blood.

   *b*) The appropriation of God's righteousness. Not only does the death of Christ give Him the right to declare us righteous before God, but He makes the righteousness of God part of us. God's nature becomes our nature when we believe on the Lord Jesus Christ (2 Cor. 5:21).

B. The Person who came is described by the term "Christ Jesus," "Christ" being His divine name, and "Jesus" His human name.

  1. The first time the name "Christ Jesus" occurs in this order and not "Jesus Christ" is in Acts 19:4 and thereafter it is seen in the epistles beginning with Romans 3:24. It never occurs in the Gospels because they primarily focus on the time before His resurrection.

  2. Had Jesus Christ been born into the world and died like every other human being without rising from the dead, then news of His coming would not be "worthy of all acceptation" (1 Tim. 1:15).

  3. Observe that Paul does not say that He was born of the virgin Mary, but that He came (*élthen*, voluntarily and of His own power He entered into the world). This could never be said of any other human being who ever walked upon the face of this earth. A son of Mary, if he were nothing else but that, could never have saved the soul of anyone. He is able to save sinners because He, the eternal Son

127

of God, voluntarily and of His own power came into the world.

C. Such a declaration about the justification and the simultaneous sanctification of the sinner is indeed worthy of all acceptance.

1. The Greek word for acceptance is *apodoché*, which occurs only in 1 Timothy 1:15 and 4:9. This word comes from the preposition *apó*, "from," and *déchomai*, "to accept." It means to embrace, to receive with joy and approval as something very precious and worthwhile.

2. The complete phrase, ". . . a faithful saying and worthy of all acceptation," is exactly the same in 1 Timothy 1:15 and 4:9.

   *a)* 1 Timothy 1:15 undoubtedly refers to the purpose of the incarnation of God in the Person of Christ Jesus, the salvation of sinners. It means that sinners should place their full trust in accepting God's plan. The phrase further affirms that the results promised—being pronounced justified before God and being given God's nature—are absolutely trustworthy.

   *b)* In 1 Timothy 4:9 the phrase stands in contrast to the profane and old wives' fables of verse seven. It is as if the apostle Paul is stating that the incarnation of Jesus Christ is not a fable. The "old wives tales" may be false, but what Jesus promised to do—through His incarnation, His life, His death, and His resurrection—He would fulfill.

3. "Of all acceptation" declares that this is absolutely trustworthy. You can be absolutely sure that when you come to Jesus Christ in humility and in repentance, He will forgive you of your sin and He will give you victory over sin, making you a new creature in Him (2 Cor. 5:17).

# God Desires All People To Be Saved

Key Verse: 1 Timothy 2:4

## I. Paul Urges Prayer for Others

A. There is no one whom God's grace cannot reach. Paul exhorts Timothy to pray for "all men" (1 Tim. 2:1), having just described how God saved him, "chief" of sinners (1 Tim. 1:15).

B. He urges prayer also for all in authority that we may lead a quiet and peaceable life in all godliness and honesty (1 Tim. 2:2). God has ordained political authority for our benefit (Rom. 13:1–7).

## II. God Is the Only Savior

A. Some are tempted to look to earthly rulers as "saviors" instead of God (1 Tim. 2:3, 5).

B. Scripture teaches that no one beside God can truly save us (Mark 2:7). Before the incarnation, the angel announced to Joseph that Jesus was going to "save his people from their sins" (Matt. 1:21). Likewise, the virgin Mary sang in the Magnificat, "and my spirit hath rejoiced in God my Savior" (Luke 1:47). These were acknowledgments that Jesus' primary function for coming into the world the first time was to save man (John 3:17).

C. God's ability to save is not limited (1 Tim. 2:4, 6). We must never reduce Him to a human savior who may be either incapable or undesirous of saving.

D. His invitation is to all; He loves all and invites all (John 3:16; Matt. 11:28). He will not turn away anyone who comes to Him for salvation (John 6:37).

III. **God's Salvation Is Available to All, but Not All Will Accept It**

    A. In all of creation, only man is made in the image and likeness of God (Gen. 1:26) with a moral awareness.

    B. Ever since Adam and Eve chose to disobey God in the Garden of Eden (Gen. 3:16, 17), men have continued to sin, "For all have sinned and come short of the glory of God" (Rom. 3:23).

    C. Because of His great love (John 3:16), God wills (*thélei* in 1 Tim. 2:4) that some be saved, as in the case of the unwilling Saul (Acts 9:5).

    D. Note in John 6:37 that there is a condition given, "All that the Father giveth me shall come to me." Jesus repeats this stipulation in John 10:26–30 in the imagery of the shepherd and the sheep.

    E. Although God desires that all people come to Him (2 Pet. 3:9), He only chooses some (John 15:16) because He knows who they are (Rom. 8:29). That is why Paul so earnestly entreats Timothy to petition God for all men.

# Godliness and Money

Key Verse: 1 Timothy 6:6

---

## I. What Godliness Is and Is Not!

A. How is godliness described? In English the word "God" is part of the word "godliness," but in Greek *eusébeia*, from which godliness is translated (Acts 3:12; 1 Tim. 2:2; 3:16; 4:7, 8; 6:3, 5, 6, 11; 2 Tim. 3:5; Titus 1:1; 2 Pet. 1:3, 6, 7; 3:11), does not contain the word "god." The opposite is *asébeia* (Rom. 1:18; 11:26; 2 Tim. 2:16; Titus 2:12; Jude 1:15, 18) translated "ungodliness" or "without reverence."

1. The word is derived from *eu*, "good or well," and *sébomai*, a verb meaning "to reverence, venerate, worship" (Matt. 15:9; Mark 7:7; Acts 13:43, 50; 16:14; 17:4, 17; 18:7, 13; 19:27).

   *a*) The basic meaning of the word is simply to have good respect.

   *b*) The opposite is *asebéō*, "to act or live in an ungodly or irreverent manner" (2 Pet. 2:6; Jude 1:15).

2. *Eusébeia* is piety or reverence directed toward God. It denotes the spontaneous feeling of the heart, thus differing from *eulábeia* (Heb. 5:7; 12:28) which is caution, circumspection, fear of God.

   *a*) The adjective *eusebḗs* means to be religious, devout toward God, pious (Acts 10:2, 7; 22:12; 2 Pet. 2:9; Sept.: Is. 24:16; 26:7). The opposite is *asebḗs*, "ungodly or disrespectful" (Rom. 4:5; 5:6; 1 Tim. 1:9; 1 Pet. 4:18; 2 Pet. 2:5; 3:7; Jude 1:4, 15). The adverb *eusebṓs* (2 Tim. 3:12; Titus

2:12) means piously, religiously. The verb *eusebéō* (Acts 17:23; 1 Tim. 5:4) means to be pious or respectful toward anyone as toward God, meaning to respect, to honor.

b) The stem *seb*, which is the root of all these words, means "to fall back or forward." Such bodily movement was the expression of an inner attitude of reverence.

3. There is a Greek word, however, that combines the word "God," *theós*, with *sébomai* (1 Tim. 2:10) and means reverence toward God or godliness. This word, the adjective *theosebḗs*, (John 9:31; Sept.: Ex. 18:26; Job 1:1, 8) means "reverencing God," godly, a worshiper of God. The opposite of *theosebḗs*, "godly," is *theostugḗs*, "impious, hating God" (Rom. 1:30).

4. Due to the fact that *eusébeia* (see A above) in the New Testament always refers to respect toward God, it has been translated as "godliness" albeit the word itself in Greek does not include the word "God." Therefore, the word *eusebḗs* can be taken as synonymous with *theosébeia* indicating that the *eu*, "good," is synonymous with God. "Good respect" in the New Testament means reverence toward God and no one else.

B. In the New Testament the word *eusébeia*, "godliness or proper reverence," is not the same as justification by faith through Jesus Christ (Rom. 3:24, 26, 28; 5:1, 9).

1. Godliness was not the new birth which the Lord Jesus was eager for Nicodemus to have.

a) Nicodemus, like Cornelius (one a Jew, the other a Gentile), was indeed *eusebḗs*, "reverencing God," but he was not born again. Therefore, one can be godly and not be saved, but you cannot be saved and be ungodly. Both the ungodly (*asebēs*) and the godly (*eusebēs*) need to be saved.

  b) Cornelius was *eusebēs*, "godly." He was a deeply religious person (Acts 10:30), but he was saved only when Peter came to him and the Holy Spirit did the work of conviction. He was baptized first into the body of Christ and then in water (Acts 10:43–48). When this took place Cornelius and the other Gentiles present at Caesarea "held their peace, and glorified God, saying, 'Then hath God also to the Gentiles granted repentance unto life'" (Acts 11:18). Thus one can be a godly Jew or Gentile person and yet be unsaved.

C. *Eusébeia* is a life that is respectful toward God and His laws.

  1. This godliness or piety may be one's natural inclination. We call such people religious.

  2. Such "godly" people may be saved or unsaved.

    a) If they are saved, their reverential attitude toward God is the result of their justificaton by faith through Jesus Christ (Rom. 5:1; Gal. 5:22, 23).

    b) Even the unsaved may live moral and exemplary lives. However, their manner of life can never become the means of their justification by God. Salvation is only attained by faith in Jesus Christ and His work on Calvary for us. Good works without faith are useless and faith without works is dead (Eph. 2:8, 9; James 2:17).

## II. Godliness and the Believer's Conduct

A. Godliness is a vital part of the believer's conduct.

  1. Paul speaks in the pastoral epistles nine times about this *eusébeia*, "the godliness or reverential external

behavior of the believer" (1 Tim. 2:2; 3:16; 4:7, 8; 6:3, 5, 6, 11; 2 Tim. 3:5; Titus 1:1).

2. This godliness is the product of living faith in Christ. For a believer, it is the outward manifestation of an inward experience.

B. Godliness is a beneficial part of the believer's conduct.

1. The believer is better off by externally upholding God and His Word and laws than what he may think best for himself. "Godliness with contentment is great gain" (1 Tim. 6:6).

a) The word translated "gain" is *porismós* (only in 1 Tim. 6:5, 6), not the common Greek word *kérdos* (Phil. 1:21; 3:7; Titus 1:11), meaning "profit or advantage that is to be realized or has already been realized." *Porismós*, however, is "the means of acquiring gain."

(1) It is derived from *póros* which originally meant "a means of passage over a river, a ford or ferry, a pathway, a way."

(2) This is the word from which we get our English word "pore" (a passage or channel, usually microscopic as in plants, leaves, or skin). Also, the adjective "porous" is derived from it which means something that has tiny holes through which an element can pass or breathe, so to speak. *Porismós* indicates the means whereby one may have a need provided.

2. Living reverentially toward God does not prohibit the Christian from acquiring the necessities of life.

a) One need not disregard God and His moral laws in order to make a living.

b) Financial, political, and social success is possible for the Christian as he fully reverences God.

3. There is a qualification for godliness (*eusébeia*) if it

is to be a means of provision of earthly good: godliness must be "with contentment" (v. 6).

    *a*) The Greek word translated "contentment" is *autárkeia*, "self-sufficiency as a mind-set."

    *b*) Quantity of acquisitions does not of itself bring joy in life. Rather, it is the attitude of considering what one gains as sufficient to meet his needs for the time being. Future acquisitions must never steal from the present joy of thanking God for whatever one has as sufficient for his needs.

4. When one's conduct in acquiring material things honors God, he has a satisfaction which "acquisitions" on their own can never give.

    *a*) This is the meaning of the adjective "great" (v. 6).

    *b*) "Great" does not refer to the amount of profits or material gain, but to the satisfaction which the inner man derives from his external riches.

## III. The Curse of Money or Acquisitions Without Godliness

A. There are people who are rich and miserable and others who are rich and inwardly satisfied.

1. What provides or removes this satisfaction in possessions?

2. The determining factors are the principles adhered to in the acquisition of possessions.

B. Such enrichment based on evil principles is described in 1 Timothy 6:5 which stands in contrast to the next verse.

1. The evil principles are described as "Perverse disputings of men of corrupt minds."

    *a*) "Perverse disputings" refers to the constancy of their improper approaches to godliness.

    *b*) "Men of corrupt minds" refers to those who try to rationalize devious means of enrichment instead of maintaining godly conduct.

*c)* Paul further describes these men as "destitute of the truth." They set aside the truth they know about godly behavior.

2. Their wrong approach Paul expresses as "supposing that gain is godliness." These are the people who mistakenly think that godliness is a means to acquiring riches. The translation should be, "supposing that godliness is profiteering." Who are these who profiteer from being religious?

   *a)* The merchant becomes a member of a church so that he may make acquaintances in order to sell his products. His external piety is not real but has the ulterior motive of enrichment.

   *b)* The preacher or Christian worker paid to do a full-time job may neglect his duty. Often this "minister" travels around, preaching in other places, rationalizing his actions because he is "preaching the gospel."

      (1) Too often his eye is on how large the "love offering" will be. Like the merchant, his focus is on serving himself, not God.

      (2) The situation becomes worse if he rationalizes the offering (or gift) as nontaxable and thus never declares it as income. Recent history provides numerous examples of this sad practice.

C. That is what Paul calls godliness which "corrupts" (*kapēleúō* which means "to treat as if for personal profit"; found only in 2 Cor. 2:17).

   1. Our desire to profiteer from the word of God corrupts it. Let us beware of "godliness" for the purpose of material gain.

   2. Did not Jesus specifically warn us in Mark 8:36, "For what shall it profit a man, if he shall gain the whole world, and lose his own soul?"

# Feel Rich with What You Have

Key Verse: 1 Timothy 6:6

---

I. **Some Feign Godliness for the Sake of Personal Gain**
   A. As in the days of Paul, so today there are those who pretend to be teachers of the Bible for the sake of personal enrichment, ". . . supposing that gain is godliness . . ." (1 Tim. 6:5). This means that there are those who use outward piety for selfish purposes.
   B. The word for "godliness" is *eusébeia*, meaning "the external manifestation of religious devotion." The opposite of this outer expression of faith is *eulábeia*, "the inner reception of God's peace" (John 14:27).
   C. Outward piety can be valid if one is sincerely seeking to please God. However, Paul warns against those who teach for the sake of personal profit, "For they that are such serve not our Lord Jesus Christ, but their own belly; and by good words and fair speeches deceive the hearts of the simple" (Rom. 16:18).
   D. Such preachers teach a different gospel (*heterodidaskalía*, "teach otherwise" in 1 Tim. 6:3). In reality they are "proud." The Greek word is *tetúphōtai*, "one who throws up a smokescreen to deceive others about himself" (1 Tim. 6:4).
   E. They are men of corrupt minds, who are "destitute of the truth" (1 Tim. 6:5), teaching a health and wealth gospel and thus becoming enemies of the cross of Christ (Phil. 3:18).
   F. Church leaders are exhorted not to be desirous of

"filthy lucre" by Peter (1 Pet. 5:2) and Paul (1 Tim. 3:8; Titus 1:7).

G. ". . . From such withdraw thyself" (1 Tim. 6:5). To support or join with such teachers is to also participate in their pretense.

## II. There Are Others Who Practice True Godliness

A. The same word, *eusébeia*, used in 1 Timothy 6:5 to refer to false piety, is also employed in verse six to describe true godliness.

B. Such commendable piety comes when one is satisfied with what he has: "But godliness with contentment is great gain" (1 Tim. 6:6). The word translated "contentment" in Greek is *autárkeia*, "to deem sufficient whatever one has." The opposite of *autárkeia* is *pleonexía*, "the desire to have more than what one possesses." The only other place *autárkeia* occurs is 2 Corinthians 9:8, where one who has "sufficiency" is described as being able to share with others. The best givers are not necessarily those who have plenty, but rather those who consider what they have to be enough for themselves and others also.

## III. You Can Become Truly Rich

A. The desire of gain (*porísmós*) is innate in man. He can either fulfill this desire honestly or by evil means. 1 Timothy 6:5 admonishes us not to use external piety as a means of personal profit. This teaching does not contradict what Paul teaches in 1 Timothy 5:18, "the laborer is worthy of his reward." The word "reward" here is not *porismós*, but *misthós*, "pay for work done." Such money is honestly acquired.

B. The gain commended in 1 Timothy 6:6 is described as "great." It is acquired as a consequence of our contentment with what God has given us and our desire to share it with others.

# Death Should Not Frighten Us

Key Verse: 2 Timothy 2:11

---

I. **As Paul Wrote This Letter He Was Facing Death**
   A. The Book of 2 Timothy was written in prison just before Paul's execution by Nero. He knew that such a death might also befall his son in the faith, Timothy, as well as any other faithful servant of Christ.
   B. Nevertheless, Paul's concern was not for his own life but for the furtherance of the gospel (2 Tim. 2:9, 10).

II. **His Encouragement to Timothy Was That Christ "Was Raised from the Dead" (2 Tim. 2:8)**
   A. The verb *egēgerménon* is the perfect passive participle with a middle meaning, one who has raised Himself from the dead. It refers to Christ's historic resurrection and the fact that He is alive today holding "the keys of hell and of death" (Rev. 1:18).
   B. In this instance Paul refers to the Lord as Jesus Christ, stressing His humanity first (only after Jesus' resurrection was He called Christ Jesus, emphasizing His divinity). It is possible that Paul wanted to remind Timothy that he too might be required to die like Jesus. But just as He rose from the dead, so also Christ promises eternal life to those who follow Him (1 Cor. 15:22, 23).

III. **Suffering for Christ Was in Accordance with the Gospel Paul Preached**

A. Paul did not preach a gospel of health and prosperity. On the contrary, Jesus instructed His disciples that they would have trials in this world (John 15:20). This was especially true for Paul as an apostle (Acts 9:16).

B. Paul's gospel was one of suffering: "Wherein I suffer trouble . . ." (2 Tim. 2:9). The verb used is *kakopathō*, which means "to suffer evils." In 2 Timothy 4:5, Paul commands Timothy to suffer evil (*kakopátheson*), or "endure afflictions."

IV. **Our Rewards in Heaven Will Be Commensurate with Our Faithfulness on Earth**

A. "For if we be dead with him, we shall also live with him" (2 Tim. 2:11). This does not refer to our involuntarily being put to death, but rather to our willingness to sacrifice for Christ (Matt. 16:24). To the extent that we bear our cross in this life we shall be rewarded in the next.

B. Jesus taught this truth in the parable of the laborers (Matt. 20:1–16) and that of the faithful and bad servant (Matt. 24:45–51; Luke 12:36–48). Our entrance into heaven, however, will be based solely on our acceptance of Christ's sacrifice for us.

# What Is the Crown of Righteousness?

Key Verse: 2 Timothy 4:8

---

I. **What Types of Crowns Are There?**
   A. There are two separate words for "crown" in Greek.
      1. The first is *stéphanos* which refers to the wreath given by the Greeks to the winner of an athletic game as a mark of victory, or to symbolize military prowess, or honor civil service. It was worn on festive occasions or at funerals (the Romans used the term *coróna* in the same way for crowns made of many different materials which acknowledged a variety of achievements).
      2. A second Greek word, *diádēma*, signifies the official headdress of a king or a priest and is derived from the Greek verb, *diadéō*, "to bind." Therefore, it denotes an inherited royalty or priesthood while *stéphanos* signifies a reward for victory or honor achieved.
   B. Which kind of crown did the Roman soldiers place on Jesus' head?
      1. Since they mockingly crowned Him king of the Jews, what they placed on His head should have been called a diadem; but instead it was called a *stéphanos* (Matt. 27:29; Mark 15:17; John 19:2, 5).
      2. This designation demonstrated the common belief by Jesus' enemies that the crucifixion was not the hour of victory for Him. They meant it derisively to indicate that they had defeated Him. But little

did they realize that they were really proclaiming the truth by placing a *stéphanos* on His head because He was indeed going to rise triumphantly from the grave.

## II. Which Crown Will the Believer Wear?

A. All believers in this life and in the one to come, wear a diadem of their King and High Priest, Christ Jesus (Rev. 1:6).

B. Likewise, Paul declares to Timothy that Jesus Christ is righteous and will justly reward each believer with a *stéphanos* for his faithful service to Christ on earth.

C. No suffering for Christ will go unrewarded.

1. Although Paul was in prison when he wrote 2 Timothy, he did not bemoan his imprisonment for Christ because he knew he would be recompensed.

2. He did not consider physical death a defeat but a victory as had his Master. In verse six he says, "for I am now ready to be offered. . . ." The verb that he uses is *spéndomai*, which means "I pour out myself," referring to his own blood being an offering to Christ.

3. He emphasizes to Timothy, and to us, that his whole life has been a fight, a struggle which has consumed his energy, "I have fought a good fight, I have finished my course, I have kept the faith" (v. 7).

4. He knew that the reward of the believer is never complete here on earth. "Henceforth" means hereafter, in the future. The phrase "there is laid up for me" implies that God has made a personal deposit in Paul's eternal account that he will receive someday. This reward will be a *stéphanos* exclusively for Paul.

## III. When Will the Crown of Righteousness Be Awarded?

A. Paul specifies it as "at that day." There is a day in the future when all those who belong to Christ will appear before his *bēma*, or "tribunal" (2 Cor. 5:10) to be rewarded for their faith (1 Cor. 5:5; 2 Cor. 1:14; Phil. 1:6, 10; 2:16; 2 Thess. 2:2). In 2 Timothy 1:12, 18; 4:8 this judgment is referred to as "that day."

B. Those who have faithfully contended on behalf of Christ will naturally be looking forward to His appearing. On the other hand, why should other believers anticipate a day when they have nothing coming to them?

# Paul Did Not Practice Selfishness

Key Verse: Philemon 1:12

## I. Paul and Philemon Were Brothers in the Lord
A. While Paul was in jail for preaching the gospel, he wrote to Philemon who had been converted under Paul's preaching and now had a church meeting in his house in Colosse (Col. 4:9; Phile. 1:2, 19).
B. Paul wrote concerning Onesimus, whose name means "profitable." Onesimus had formerly been a slave of Philemon, but after escaping to Rome, he was converted under Paul's preaching (Phile. 1:10). Although Paul greatly valued Onesimus, he felt obliged to have him return to his former owner (Phile. 1:11, 12).

## II. There Had Been a Break in the Relationship Between Philemon and Onesimus
A. In all probability, Onesimus had left his master before becoming a Christian.
B. Philemon may have also been an unbeliever at the time of Onesimus' disappearance.

## III. Restoration Is a Must in the Life of Faith
A. After both men became believers, it was necessary that they be reconciled to each other (Eph. 4:31; Heb. 12:15).
B. Christ Himself stressed the need to make amends with others before worshiping God (Matt. 5:23, 24). Thus, Onesimus' desire to obey the Lord Jesus overcame his fear of being returned to slavery.

C. Paul was very careful not to assert his authority in his request to Philemon to receive Onesimus now, not as a slave, but as a brother (Phile. 1:14–16).

IV. **Paul Acted Totally Unselfishly in His Dealings with Philemon Concerning Onesimus**

A. Paul could have rationalized that he was entitled to keep Onesimus to serve him since he had won him to Christ. Paul, however, realized that it was more important that Onesimus be reconciled to Philemon. Are we equally unselfish in our service for the Lord?

B. Paul did not delay doing what he felt was his immediate duty. He could have waited to bring Onesimus to Philemon after he became free to travel to Colosse. Or he might have invited Philemon to Rome to visit Onesimus and himself. In the meantime, he would have had the service of Onesimus. It is always tempting to delay obedience to the Lord when it seems that it will be to our advantage.

C. Paul even offered to repay any debts Onesimus might have owed Philemon in order to insure his freedom.

# Our Glorification Through Suffering

Key Verse: Hebrews 2:10

---

I. **Is Life without Suffering a Blessing or a Curse?**
   A. A blessing is what causes us to come closer to God, our Creator, and Jesus Christ, our Redeemer.
   B. The joys of life are not found in possessions but in relationships (Luke 12:15; John 17:3).
   C. If Christ is first in one's life, material things are not excluded, but they must be secondary; otherwise Christ can never be to us what He wants to be.
   D. Review your life at the end of the year and ask yourself: Have I been closer to the Lord? If not, have I sought prosperity more than Him or have I looked at prosperity as a means to make Him known?

II. **The Cross Was Christ's Crowning Experience**
   A. This is the subject of Hebrews chapter two:
      "Jesus . . . for the suffering of death crowned with glory and honor, that he by the grace of God should taste death for every man" (v. 9).
   B. "For it became him, for whom are all things, and by whom are all things, in bringing many sons unto glory, to make the captain of their salvation perfect through sufferings" (v. 10).
      1. Who is "him" in the phrase, "For it became him"? It is God. He made "the captain of their salvation perfect through sufferings." The captain of salvation is Christ as "high priest," who shed His blood for the sins of the people (2:17; 9:12, 14).

2. This speaks of the necessity and propriety of the cross for Christ. The word "became" in the phrase "For it became him" is the word *éprepe* in Greek, the imperfect of *prépō*, which is used in the New Testament in its impersonal form *prépei*, it is "fitting, proper, right, and consequently necessary." God had externally decreed that man's salvation could be accomplished only thrugh the shedding of blood by One who was sinless. The only other instance of the use of *éprepen* is Hebrews 7:26: "For such a high priest became [*éprepen*, 'right, fitting, proper, necessary'] us, who is holy, harmless, undefiled, separate from sinners, and made higher than the heavens." It was fitting for Him to die because He was without sin (Heb. 4:15), while we are all sinners (Rom. 3:23). The imperfect tense indicates that the sacrifice of Jesus Christ had been determined by God from the very beginning. It was not a decision within time and space. There could be no other means of redemption of the human race.

3. The "sufferings" referred to here are what led to Christ's death on the cross (vv. 9, 10). It was not cruelty nor foolishness on the part of God to allow the just to die for the unjust (1 Pet. 3:18). The Jews considered the cross a stumblingblock and the Greeks considered it foolishness (1 Cor. 1:23).

    *a)* The Jews expected a triumphant Messiah. They had no room for a cross. The Jews would have found it far easier to accept Christ if there had been no mention of rejection, shame, and death in the story of His life. Even the triumph of His resurrection did not remove the difficulties of the cross from their minds. They would have accepted Him if He had proceeded from the "Hosannas" of the triumphal entry to the glory of the Ascension, avoiding Golgotha altogether.

One does not have either to explain or understand that which God the Creator ordained to come to pass. The Epistle to the Hebrews and Paul's epistles were written to extol the glory of the cross, which the Jews thought a shame and the Greeks thought foolishness. Christ's cross was His crown of glory and honor (Heb. 2:7). Whenever we do that which is right, proper, and morally necessary, even if it results in suffering and death, it is a crown of glory and honor for us. That is the way to look upon the sufferings resulting from the execution of moral duty.

b) "For it was proper, fitting . . . to make perfect [*teleiōsai*, aorist infinitive active of *teleióō*] . . . to bring to His goal, to accomplish His purpose." The NASB says "to perfect" and the NIV, "should make . . . perfect." The danger with these translations is that Jesus Christ may be thought of as imperfect until such time as He died for our sin (Rom. 5:6, 8; 1 Cor. 15:3). Jesus rather reached the end, the purpose of His incarnation when on the cross He cried, "It is finished." The word in Greek is *tetélestai*, the perfect indicative passive of *teleō*, meaning "to finish, to end, to complete." The death of Christ was the completion of the purpose of His incarnation by the necessity of suffering and death.

c) Jesus Christ is here called "the captain of their salvation." The Greek word is *archēgón*, from *archế*, "beginning," and *ágō*, "to lead." In Acts 3:15 *archēgós* is translated "prince" with reference to life. In Hebrews 12:2, *archēgós* is translated "author . . . of our faith." The word *archēgós* is explained by Hebrews 5:9, where the word translated "author" is *aítios*, meaning "causes," referring to the personal cause of eternal salvation. Jesus Christ is the absolute cause of salvation, life, and faith.

## III. Jesus Christ Is the Savior of the Created World

A. The verb "are" is not in the Greek, taking the statement out of the context of time. There has never been anytime when this was, is, and will not be true. Forever all things are for Christ and by or through Him. This is an eternal truth, valid before His incarnation, during it and following it.

B. "For Him" means for His glory and "through Him" refers to His sustaining power. Glory is the revelation of His essence, that He has always been God in spite of His humiliation unto death (Phil. 2:6–8). His power is what sustains everything (Col. 1:17). He, through whom everything holds together, gave Himself to die on the cross, the humiliating mode of death.

C. "All things" in Greek is *tá pánta*, (see also Heb. 2:8) and means not only all things, but all creatures, every one individually and all of them put together. The statement is not qualified by any verb. There can be no greater statement as to the absoluteness, deity and sovereignty of the Lord Jesus, in spite of His death and sufferings. Had He died as man only He could not have been the author of our salvation, but He died as the God-Man (Mark 2:10). If deity at all times is not attributed to Jesus Christ, He cannot be an effective Savior from sin.

## IV. How Effective Was Christ's Death in ". . . Bringing Many Sons unto Glory . . ."?

A. "In bringing" in Greek is *agagónta*, the aorist participle of *ágō*, "to lead." At a particular time in the past Christ, through His death, was not only Himself crowned with glory and honor, but He accomplished the same for many humans. Jesus Christ's death was His hour of glorification, the hour of understanding who and what He really was (John 12:16, 23, 28; 13:31, 32; 14:13; 15:8).

B. Through His death, Christ led (*agagónta*) to glory "many sons." His death led to His resurrection. He is the "firstborn from the dead" (Col. 1:18; Rev. 1:5), and our death as believers is gain because it is the first step in the process of our glorification. We shall be with Him (Phil 1:21, 23); we shall come back with Him to an earth that is changed (1 Thess. 3:13; Rev. 21:1), where righteousness dwells (2 Pet. 3:13), and where we shall judge the world (1 Cor. 6:2). Think of the glory of judging those who now oppress us!

C. This glorification of the believer is first because of the sufferings of Christ. Yet it is not going to be enjoyed by all believers but each in proportion to his sufferings on the behalf of Christ. There is only one passage of Scripture where the word *sundoxasthōmen*, "to glorify together," occurs in the New Testament, Romans 8:17: "And if children, then heirs; heirs of God, and joint-heirs with Christ, if so be that we suffer with him, that we may be also glorified together."

D. The particular glorification of which the Apostle speaks in Hebrews 2:10 is not for all sons of God, but for many. The Greek word is *polloús*, which here cannot be taken as "all." It is as many as have suffered with Him that He will proportionately glorify with Him. Those who, as His children, are conformed to the will of their heavenly Father, will be glorified in the measure that they were willing to suffer with and for Christ. Therefore, the greatest blessing in life is not how much we are able to prosper, but how much we have been able rejoicingly to suffer with and for Christ.

# How to Fight in Order to Win

Key Verse: Hebrews 12:1

---

I. **When Should a Christian Fight?**
   A. There is no virtue in mere fighting. One who fights for the sake of fighting wastes his life.
   B. Fighting must have a cause to be worthwhile.
   C. Fighting is necessary for the Christian because of the entrance and reign of sin in our world (Rom. 5:12).
   D. A person who does not fight for or against anything is a person who stands for nothing.
      1. Because there are those who have no principles, those who have principles must stand up against them.
      2. Our world is divided into those who insist on being enemies of God and those who have made their peace with God (Rom. 5:1). Because both evil and good exist in our world, fighting is inevitable. This is one kind of fighting.
   E. A second kind could better be termed a race for excellence among those who are in general agreement. The unbelievers are in a race to see who will accomplish more evil and the believers are in another race to see who will please Christ the most.
   F. This is what it is called in Hebrews 12:1, ". . . let us run . . . the race." That word translated "race" in Greek is *agón*, from which *agónizomai* is derived, the equivalent of the English "to agonize." The same Greek word is what we render in English as "fight" and "race" or "an endeavor to be first, to excel." Both

meanings can have a good and a bad connotation. If the motive is right then it is good. Fighting evil for the glory of God is good. Fighting your brother to put him down so you can be proud of being first is evil. However, if you are striving for excellence to stimulate others to follow your example, then running in a competitive race is good. The word *agṓn*, "fight" or "race" is derived from the verb *ágō*, "to lead." At first *agṓn* meant "a gathering of people." Later it came to mean a place of assembly and then a contest, conflict.

## II. The Christian Life Is a Conflict

A. Examine the lives of saints of God in the past and you will see that every one of them had a conflict. These are enumerated in Hebrews chapter eleven: Abel, Enoch, Noah, Abraham, Sarah, Isaac, Jacob, Esau, Joseph, Moses, Rahab, Gideon, Barak, Samson, Jephthah, David, Samuel.
   1. None were exempt from conflicts and sufferings.
   2. The conflicts occurred because of the presence of sin in the world, their own yet unredeemed bodies, and the presence of other yet "imperfect" people in their family and communal surroundings.

B. Our world has not changed.
   1. These same circumstances surround us in spite of Christ's coming into the world.
   2. There will be conflicts as long as we live since we are not an island unto ourselves. Communal living means inevitable conflict.

C. Their work will remain incomplete unless we shoulder our responsibility in the conflict. Observe how the eleventh chapter of Hebrews ends, "God having provided some better thing for us, that they [the saints of the past] without us [you and me] should not be made perfect." That phrase "be made perfect" (*teleiōthōsi*)

means that their work could not be completed without
our labor for God.

## III. Why Should We Join in the Conflict?
A. If you and I are determined to avoid conflict we will
not do what needs to be done.
B. What we have to do puts the finishing touches on
what others have done.
C. If they did what they did because it was their God-
given responsibility, and consequently took the heat
for it, so must we.
D. You and I cannot do anything worthwhile without
engaging in conflict and the concomitant sufferings.
E. The teaching that Christianity is a walk in a rosy gar-
den is unscriptural. It is instead peace in the heart in
spite of the conflict around us (John 16:33). It is peace
between God and us and a peaceful attitude (Rom.
14:19; 1 Cor. 1:3; 7:15; Eph. 6:23). However, the attitude of others toward God may affect this peace.
When others are slothful in their work, we ought to
move forward, not rejoicing in leaving them behind,
but encouraging them to move forward with us. Let us
concentrate on running the race that is set before us.

## IV. How Must We Fight?
A. We must not fight sitting down, nor walking, but
running. Life is a race. Only he who runs gets to the
goal first.
B. If we do not reach the goal, it means we did not run.
It is never too late to start.
C. "Let us run" in Greek is *tréchōmen*, in the present subjunctive which means:
1. It is a present duty. We can never say, "I ran and I
reached my goal."

2. It is a continuous race. Every goal reached reveals another loftier goal to be reached.

3. It is a personal responsibility.

D. We cannot run if we are burdened with unnecessary weights.

1. Try picking up one hundred pounds and start running. You will not get very far.

2. Put off every "malignant tumor." The word for "weight" is *ógkos* or *ónkos* from which is derived the English "oncology," the study of tumors. There are malignant tumors that attack our healthy spiritual organisms. We should examine ourselves for spiritual tumors. The sooner we discover them and have them excised, the faster we can run the race. Be careful lest any habit become a malignant tumor. The word *ógkos* does not occur anywhere else in the New Testament.

3. Let us put off sin.

*a)* There are certain sins that are all around us, common among men. This is the idea behind the Greek word *euperístatos* (derived from *perístamai*, "to stand around"), translated "which doth so easily beset us." It is the sin that stands around us. Watch the sin which "everybody" else does and rationalizes. Just because no one else reaches the goal does not mean that you should not. Beware of "common sins."

*b)* The prefix of the word *euperístatos* (*eu*, "well, thoroughly") further emphasizes the thorough danger of the sins that are so common around us. The deceptions of a common sin are that it looks good and that "everyone else is doing it, so it can't be that bad." Watch out for it. If you do not you may never reach the goal.

# The Temporal and the Eternal

Key Verse: Hebrews 12:26

---

I. **Nothing Ever Vanishes**
   A. Nothing that is created ever vanishes. When something is burned it becomes ashes, changing from one form of existence into another.
   B. This is the truth which helps us to understand certain misconceived words of the New Testament.
      1. "To destroy, to lose, to perish" are all translations of *apóllumi*. It does not mean to cease to exist, but to ruin so as to make something unable or unfit to accomplish what it was made for, such as the wineskins (Luke 5:37). It means to lose possession of someone or something. The shepherd could not find the sheep but the sheep still existed (Luke 15:4, 6). Likewise, the son was lost to the father, even though he still existed (Luke 15:24). The same is true of the perishing of food (John 6:27), gold (1 Pet. 1:7), persons (Matt. 2:13; 8:25; 22:7; 27:20), and the well-being of the unsaved in the hereafter (Matt. 10:28; Luke 13:5; John 3:16; 10:28; 17:12; Rom. 2:12). Also the noun *apóleia* is often translated "destruction" (Matt. 7:13; Rom. 9:22; Phil. 3:19; 2 Pet. 2:1; 3:16), "perdition" (John 17:12; Phil. 1:28; 2 Thess. 2:3; 1 Tim. 6:9; Heb. 10:39; 2 Pet. 3:7; Rev. 17:8, 11), "waste" (Matt. 7:26; Mark 14:4).

2. *Katalúō*, commonly translated "destroy," never means to render extinct. It derives from *katá*, "down," or as an intensive, and *lúō*, "to loose, to bind, to demolish, dissolve." Figuratively, it means "not to apply, to loosen its binding application or obligation." The compound *katalúō* means "to dis-unite, as to dismantle a building" (Matt. 26:61; 27:40; Mark 14:58; 15:29; Acts 6:14); "to put an end to its previous purpose and goal." It is used in reference to the law (Matt. 5:17), or to a work (Acts 5:38, 39; Rom. 14:20).

3. *Olothreúō*, used only in Hebrews 11:28, is translated "destroyed," in reference to the killing of all the firstborn. Dying is the reducing of someone from one form of life, corporeal, to another, incorporeal (Luke 16:22–24; John 11:25; 12:24; Rom. 6:9; Phil. 1:21; 1 Thess. 4:14; Heb. 9:27). The same is true of the noun *ólethros* (1 Cor. 5:5; 1 Thess. 5:3; 2 Thess. 1:9; 1 Tim. 6:9).

## II. We Must Distinguish Between the Temporal and the Eternal

A. The Scriptures counsel us to distinguish between the two and attribute corresponding priorities to them.

B. Temporal things are not necessarily unimportant. The Scriptures do not say to seek only the kingdom of God, but to seek it first (Matt. 6:33). Nothing created by God is unimportant. Each thing, however, must be evaluated as to its relative importance to the permanent and remaining.

C. Paul in 2 Corinthians 4:17, 18 classifies these:

1. "For our light affliction, which is but for a moment" could better be translated "The transient thing is light and therefore easy to bear." Anything that passes is tolerable. The words translated "which

is but for a moment" are *tó parautíka,* "that which is for this very instant, the instant, the momentary, the transient thing." We would do well to recognize the transient things of life. However, even the transient things, such as affliction, will affect our permanent status: "worketh for us a far more exceeding and eternal weight of glory." So we have the transient experiences—they are light because they are transient, whereas the eternal ones are weighted with glory. Our eternal glorification will be affected by how lightly we take the transient afflictions of earth. The word eternal, *aiōnios,* ought to be connected not only with passing time but also with God Himself and the life He gives which consistently is called eternal life.

2. Paul also makes a contrast between the temporal being visibly material with the eternal things being invisibly spiritual (v. 18). To which are we giving more importance? The temporal and visible or the eternal and spiritual? Our eternal glory will be proportionate to our prioritizing the eternal and spiritual though invisible.

## III. Consider What Jesus Did

A. Jesus came to Mt. Zion in Jerusalem, the "city of the living God." What took place there produces not fear but love and worship, which are enduring.

B. One day He is coming back to Jerusalem which in every sense of the word will be heavenly in that:

1. An innumerable company of angels will be there.

2. There is going to be a festive occasion. It is too bad the word *panēguris* in Hebrews 12:22 was translated "general assembly." It is a festive convocation of the firstborn. These are those who are saved by the blood shed in Jerusalem, those whose names

are written in the book of life. These are the spirits of the just. The translation says "men made perfect." The participle is *teteleiōménōn*, the perfect passive of *teleióō*, "to reach the goal." They are those who were enabled by God to reach the final goal, to reign with Christ forever and ever.

3. Indeed, Jesus Christ shook the earth when He was being crucified (Matt. 27:51; 28:4—the same word *seiō*, "shake" is used in Heb. 12:26) but when He comes again He will shake not only the earth, but also heaven (Matt. 24:29–31).

4. This will be the final change of what is meant to be shaken, that which is temporary. Hebrews 12:26 is so inadequately translated that the reader can easily fail to see what is in it. In verse twenty-six, "Yet once more I shake [again and finally] not the earth only as I [Christ] did on my first coming." The second and final shaking is of both earth and heaven. "And this 'once more' makes manifest the mutation, the change of those things that are of shaking quality having been made that way, so that those things of not shaking quality may abide or remain" (author's translation). Those things of temporary nature will be changed to a permanent nature to coexist with the permanently external things. What a glorious translation of the temporary now visible to the eternal now invisible and then together all being made visible (Rom. 8:18–25; 1 John 3:2; Rev. 21).

# The Judgment of God

Key Verse: 1 Peter 1:17

---

## I. God's Judgment Is Certain

A. Judgment is part of the moral character of God. The meaning of the word "judge" (in Greek, *krínō*) is "to separate, divide, distinguish, discern, select, or form an opinion after evaluating a situation." God then evaluates people and situations, but His favor or disfavor may not be demonstrated immediately.

B. Judgment is immediate when we obey or disobey physical laws. If I cut myself, blood begins to flow. When dealing with spiritual laws, however, things may not happen in the same way. The mercy of God sometimes postpones the execution of judgment (2 Pet. 3:9), but this should not be understood as a cancellation of judgment. The consequence is certain.

C. The certainty of judgment in spiritual matters causes the unrewarded benefactor to continue in his good work and gives the unpunished malefactor time to think about the evil of his ways and repent.

## II. God's Judgment Is Without Partiality

A. There is nothing arbitrary about the awards given by God. His judgment is inherent in the nature of the very act of giving rewards. What we do is either good or evil. This judgment cannot be made by us; it is made by God who is absolute, as are His laws. He cannot judge individuals by different standards.

B. Our concept of God should be that of a just God. In human government we strive to see the law applied toward all without discrimination. How much more can we trust God to act impartially in spiritual matters?

C. In His fairness, God also acts as a Father. Observe how 1 Peter 1:17 begins, "And if ye call on the Father, who without respect of persons judgeth according to every man's work. . . ." That conditional particle *ei* should be translated "since" as the NIV has it: "Since you call on the Father. . . ." A true father treats each of his children justly, "without respect of persons."

## III. God's Judgment Is Christ's Judgment

A. This is clearly stated by Christ Himself in John 9:39, "For judgment I am come into this world that they which see not might see; and that they which see might be made blind." The word translated "judgment" here is not the regular *krísis*, "the act of judging in the future," but *kríma*, "the present act of judgment due to the mere presence of Jesus Christ in the world."

B. Man is judged according to his acceptance or rejection of Jesus Christ. "He that believeth on him is not condemned" (*krínetai*, "is not being judged," John 3:18). Faith in Christ Jesus then exempts a person from the judgment of God upon sin.

C. Lack of faith in Jesus Christ, conversely, calls forth God's judgment upon that person, ". . . but he that believeth not is condemned [*kékritai*, "has been judged" by his own unbelief] already, because he hath not believed in the name of the only begotten Son of God" (John 3:18).

1. He who has not exercised living, saving faith in Jesus Christ has already been judged by his own unbelief. The future judgment will only be a confirmation of a person's belief or unbelief in Christ as shown by his subsequent works.

2. ". . . the Father, who without respect of persons judgeth according to every man's work . . ." (v. 17). The verb "judgeth" is *krínonta*, the present participle of *krínō*, "to judge." Thus it refers to one judging all the time. Peter here is not referring merely to the definite future judgment (Matt. 25:31–46; Acts 10:42; 17:31; 2 Cor. 5:10; 2 Tim. 4:1), but to the constant judgment of God upon humanity and the universe.

# A Christian View of Suffering

Key Verses: 1 Peter 2:18, 19

---

I. We Sojourn in a Sinful World

    A. We should not necessarily take responsibility for the unhappy environment or circumstances in which we live. It is good, however, to examine whether our actions or inactions have in any way contributed to the state of affairs enveloping us.

    B. It is also important not to hold God responsible for affliction. God did not create the chaos and suffering in which our world is found. It is the preset and fore-ordained consequence of man's disobedience to God. If suffering did not exist, God would have proven Himself a liar in announcing the consequence of man's voluntary disobedience (Gen. 2:17; 3:17–24).

    C. We can face the evil in the world only as an individual following a conscience enlightened by God's Holy Word.

        1. It was to slaves that Peter was writing. The word "servants" in 1 Peter 2:18 is *oikétai*, "household companions," or "domestic servants living in the same house" (Luke 16:13; Acts 10:7; Rom. 14:4). We, too, were in a similar state of servitude when we became recipients of the liberating gospel of Christ and received an enlightened conscience. Jesus freed us from our sin, and it is this personal redemption that precedes and overshadows any possible future social redemption. The truth of the

matter is that it is those who are poor and socially oppressed who more readily accept Christ's "good news" of personal spiritual redemption (Luke 4:18; 7:22; James 2:5).

2. "Servants, be subject to your masters [*despótais*, meaning "despots" or "absolute rulers"] with all fear. . . ." We must carefully analyze our bosses. In coming to understand the people in authority over us, we will develop the ability to win them. The greatest achievement of a suppressed believer is not to further estrange his "despot," but to live in such a way as to cause him to inquire what it is that makes the Christian different from all the other employees. The bottom line is not for a person to "buck" the boss, but to win him. This strategy is the message of Peter to believers in his time and to all of us who may be in similar circumstances today.

## II. We Must Submit to Evil Masters

A. We must submit to evil masters as well as to those who are good. A master may be benevolent (*agathós*), and gentle or tolerant (*epieikés*, Phil. 4:5; 1 Tim. 3:3; Titus 3:2; James 3:17), or he may be crooked (*skoliós*, Luke 3:5; Acts 2:40; Phil. 2:15).

B. There are instances in which we as Christians must show reluctant tolerance toward masters from whom we cannot escape and whom we cannot change. We are, however, to submit even to "froward" masters.

## III. We Suffer in Sacrifice for the Savior

A. We must be prepared to suffer for obeying our Christian conscience. "For this is thankworthy, if a man for conscience toward God endure grief, suffering wrongfully" (1 Pet. 2:19). In the first statement, "for this is thankworthy," the latter word is translated from the Greek word *cháris*, meaning "grace." What Peter is writing about is that we are not only to obey the good and gentle masters, but also the overbearing ones. This type of circumstance requires God's grace. It is only natural for any of the redeemed to aspire to this, but God's grace is available and sufficient for such obedience.

B. To the believer God gives His conscience, *suneidésis*, or the ability to know together with God when it is sin against God to obey an earthly master and when it is not. When it comes to choosing, God must be obeyed even if it means incurring the earthly despot's wrath. He may cause grief of all kinds upon the believer, but in such cases God will give sustaining grace to him even in the full knowledge that he is suffering unjustly.

# The Beginning and the End

Key Verse: Revelation 1:8

I. There Are Three Instances in the Book of Revelation Which Declare Christ's Equality with God the Father (Rev. 1:8; 21:6; 22:13)

   A. Alpha and omega are the first and last letters of the Greek alphabet. In Hebrew, the equivalent letters are aleph and tau.

   B. These two Greek words express totality. The beginning and the end includes all in between. When we speak of someone saying, "He knows it all from A to Z," we mean he knows everything about a certain subject; he knows it from start to finish and anything in between.

II. "I Am the Alpha and Omega, the Beginning and the Ending, Saith the Lord God, Which Is, and Which Was, and Which Is to Come, the Almighty" (Revelation 1:8)

   A. Observe that this is a little different than the KJV translation which omits "God" after the word "Lord" in this verse. It should be there according to more recent editions of the Greek New Testament (e.g., the Textus Receptus and the text of the United Bible Society).

   B. John makes this as a self-declaration of God the Father. He must have heard Him say it and recorded it as he heard it.

   C. It begins with the emphatic *egō*, which in Greek is not needed to express the first person singular. In Greek, the person is indicated with the ending of the verb. In this instance it is the verb *eimí*, meaning "I am." With *egō* preceding the verb, there is added emphasis.

1. He is declaring that He is the only one who can make such a claim because it is a claim which, if not made by God Himself, must be taken as the worthless claim of a mentally deranged person.

2. This must not be taken as meaning anything less than the explanation of the same expression in Revelation 21:6 also applied to God the Father adding "the beginning and the end."

   *a)* The word "beginning" is *hē archē* which means the "origination."

   (1) This word is used in an active sense meaning the cause of everything as in Revelation 3:14 where Jesus Christ is designated as "the beginning [*hē archē*] of the creation of God." This means the cause of God's creation.

   (2) Also in John 1:1, we have the statement, "In the beginning was the Word." Here also the word *archē* occurs in its active sense. It does not refer to any particular beginning which would have required the definite article. In Greek the statement is *ēn archē*, "in beginning," and not "in the beginning" as the English translation renders it. Before there was any beginning, the Word, Christ, in His preincarnate state of self-existence, had been. The verb *ēn*, translated "was," is not an aorist past tense, but an imperfect, which would take us back from where we are to a humanly inconceivable beginning of creation when there was nothing except a self-existent God. He is called *ho Lógos*, which basically means intelligence ("logic" is

derived from *lógos*), and Word, which became the expression of God's intelligence.

*b)* The end does not mean that God will have a terminal point of His self-existence, but that just as He is the cause of all creation, He is also the one who is going to consummate His creation. This is what is called in the NT *suntéleia tou aiōnos*, of which our Lord spoke about in His eschatological statements in Matthew 13:39, 40, 49; 24:3; 28:20 (cf. Heb. 9:26). The correct meaning is "the consummation of the age." Unfortunately this important expression is mistakenly rendered as the "end of the world." *Suntéleia* is derived from *sun*, "together," and *telós*, "end." A similar word, the adjective *téleios*, "complete," is used substantively in the statement, "I am the beginning and the end [*tó téleios*]." The same God who made time and space will also bring this world of ours to a completion of its present existence and purpose. This creation will not forever remain as is. That is exactly what we have revealed in the Book of Revelation: "And I saw a new heaven and a new earth . . ." (21:1). The word new in Greek is *kainós* which means "qualitatively new."

## III. The Third Reference to Alpha and Omega Is to Jesus Christ (Rev. 22:13)

A. It is used in the context of Christ's Second Coming in glory to execute justice in distributing rewards and punishments according to our works (Rev. 22:12).

B. This "end consummation" (*télos, suntéleia*) is connected with Christ's return to earth: "Behold I am coming [*érchomai*] quickly." In this context, the word translated "quickly," *tachú*, does not mean "soon," but "suddenly, in a moment" (cf. the Greek word *atómō,* meaning in such a short, small fragment of time as to be indivisible; 1 Cor. 15:52, "in the twinkling of an eye").

## IV. Christ Being Who He Is, Can Satisfy Our Every Need

A. Observe how Revelation 2:6 closes: "I will give unto him that is athirst of the fountain of the water of life freely." That is what God can give to every one who believes on the Lord Jesus Christ as being equal with God.

B. In spite of all that man does to blaspheme and renounce Jesus, He took upon Himself the form of a servant in order to die for our sins so that we can have salvation freely, simply through faith (Eph. 2:8–10; Phil. 2:6–8).

# Index of Greek Words

This is an index of the transliterated Greek words used within the text of this book. Words are listed according to the order of the English alphabet.

| Greek | English | Scripture | Page |
|-------|---------|-----------|------|
| *adialeíptōs* | without ceasing | Rom. 2:13;<br>2 Thess. 2:13 | 104 |
| *agagónta* | led | Heb. 2:10 | 149, 150 |
| *agalliáō* | to exult | Matt. 5:12; Luke<br>1:47; 10:21; John<br>5:35; 8:56; Acts 2:26;<br>16:34; 1 Pet. 1:6, 8;<br>4:13; Rev. 19:7 | 111 |
| *agallíasis* | exultation | Luke 1:14, 44;<br>Acts 2:46; Heb. 1:9;<br>Jude 1:24 | 111 |
| *agapáō*,<br>see *agápē* | | | |
| *agápē* | love (unselfish) | John 15:9 | 40, 41, 86 |
| *agathós* | benevolence,<br>kindness | | 163 |
| *agathōsúnē* | benevolence,<br>goodness | Eph. 5:9 | 85 |
| *ágō* | to lead | | 148, 149, 152 |
| *agṓn* | contention (KJV),<br>with great struggle,<br>race | 1 Thess. 2:2<br>Heb. 12:1 | 106, 151, 152 |
| *agōnízomai*,<br>see *agṓn* | to agonize | | 151 |

169

| *aínos* | praise | Matt. 21:16;<br>Luke 18:43 | 96 |
| *aiṓn* | age, generation,<br>a kind of people | Gal. 1:4 | 72, 73, 75 |
| *aiṓnes aiṓnōn* | forever and ever,<br>the ages of the ages | (for numerous<br>references, see text) | 75 |
| *aiṓnios* | eternal | 2 Cor. 4:18 | 157 |
| *aiṓnos,*<br>see *aiṓn* | | | |
| *airéō* | to take | | 78 |
| *aítios* | author, cause | Heb. 5:9 | 148 |
| *akatharsía* | uncleanness | 1 Thess. 2:3 | 107 |
| *akoúō* | to hear | Matt. 18:17 | 8 |
| *alēthḗ* | sincere, genuine | Phil. 4:8 | 94 |
| *állos* | another | Col. 3:13 | 78, 100 |
| *aná* | up | | 100, 115 |
| *anechómenoi* | forbearing | Col. 3:13 | 100 |
| *ánesis* | rest | 2 Thess. 1:7 | 115, 116, 119 |
| *aníēmi* | to send up, let go | | 115 |
| *ánō* | up | | 115 |
| *antapodoúnai* | to repay, avenge | 2 Thess. 1:6 | 115 |
| *anthrṓpinos* | human,<br>pertaining to man | 1 Cor. 10:13 | 66 |
| *aparchḗ* | firstfruit | 1 Cor. 15:20 | 69 |
| *apéstalken* | sent | John 20:21 | 30 |

| | | | |
|---|---|---|---|
| *aphíēmi* | to remove blame, forgive, to send away from | Luke 7:42, 43; 2 Cor. 2:7, 10; 12:13 | 74, 100 |
| *apó* | from, or away from oneself | | 5, 128 |
| *apodochḗ* | to embrace, to receive with joy | 1 Tim. 1:15; 4:9 | 128 |
| *apokálupsis* | revelation | 2 Thess. 1:7 | 116 |
| *apṓleia* | perdition, die, destruction, waste | (for numerous references, see text) | 155 |
| *apóllumi* | perish, destroy, lose | (for numerous references, see text) | 155 |
| *apolúō* | dismiss | | 22 |
| *apostéllō* | to send | Matt. 10:5, 16, 40 Luke 10:1 | 30 |
| *apotássomai* | forsake | Luke 14:33 | 5 |
| *apóthesthe* | put away | Col. 3:8 | 98 |
| *archaía* | original | 2 Cor. 5:17 | 71 |
| *archḗ* | beginning, origination | Acts 11:15, 16; Rev. 21:6 | 48, 148, 166 |
| *archēgón*, see *archēgós* | | | |
| *archēgós* | captain, prince, author | Acts 3:15; Heb. 2:10; 12:2 | 148 |
| *aréskō* | to please | | 95 |
| *aretḗ* | virtue | Phil. 4:8; 2 Pet. 1:3, 5 | 95, 96 |
| *asébeia* | ungodliness, without reverence | Rom. 1:18; 11:26; 2 Tim. 2:16; Titus 2:12; 2 Pet. 2:6; Jude 1:15, 18 | 131 |

*asebéō* (verb),
see *asébeia*

| *asebés* | ungodly, disrespectful | (for numerous references, see text) | 131, 133 |
| *asélgeia* | lasciviousness | Gal. 5:21 | 87 |
| *atómō* | small fragment of time | 1 Cor. 15:52 | 168 |
| *autárkeia* | self-sufficiency, | 2 Cor. 9:8; 1 Tim. 6:6 | 135, 138 |
| *baínō* | go, proceed | | 67 |
| *baptísei* | baptize | Matt. 3:11; Mark 1:8 Luke 3:16; John 1:33 | 46 |
| *bêma* | tribunal, judgment | 2 Cor. 5:10 | 143 |
| *blastánē* | germinate, grow | Mark 4:27 | 18 |
| *blastós* | germ | | 18 |
| *bússon* | fine linen | Luke 16:19; Rev. 18:12 | 34 |

*chaírete*,
see *chaírō*

| *chaírō* | rejoice | Phil. 3:1; 4:4; Col. 1:24; 1 Thess. 3:9; 5:16 | 109, 110 |
| *chará* | joy | John 15:11; 16:20; 2 Cor. 7:4; Col. 1:11, 24; 1 Thess. 1:6; 3:9; James 1:2; 1 Pet. 4:13 | 86, 109 |
| *cháris* | grace | 1 Pet. 2:19 | 101, 109, 164 |

*charísetai*,
see *charízomai*

| | | | |
|---|---|---|---|
| *charízomai* | to give what is not deserved | Rom. 8:32 | 57 |
| *charizómenoi* | forgive | Col. 3:13 | 100 |
| *chrēstótēs* | benevolence, gentleness | Rom. 2:4; 3:12 11:22; 2 Cor. 6:6 Gal. 5:22; Eph. 2:7; Titus 3:4 | 86, 99 |
| *daimónia* | demons | Mark 16:17; Luke 10:17 | 31 |
| *dé* | (particle) and, but | Matt. 17:1; Mark 9:2; Luke 9:28 | 27 |
| *déchomai* | to accept | | 128 |
| *deí* | it is necessary | Matt. 16:21; Mark 8:31; Luke 9:22 | 19 |
| *délear* | bait | | 107 |
| *despótais* | despots, masters, absolute rulers | (for numerous references, see text) | 141 |
| *diá* | through | | 105 |
| *diádēma* | crown, kingly headdress | | 141 |
| *diadéō* | to bind | | 141 |
| *dielégeto*, see *dialégomai* | | | |
| *dialégomai* | reasoned | Acts 17:2 | 105 |
| *dikaiosúnē* | righteousness, rendering to God His rights | Eph. 5:9 | 86 |

| | | | |
|---|---|---|---|
| *dokimázontes* | testing, putting something to trial, to judge something's properness | Eph. 5:10 | 86 |
| *dokimḗ* | testing (in a positive sense) | James 1:12 | 66 |
| *dólos*, see *délear* | | | |
| *dunaménō* | power | John 10:28, 29 | 60 |
| *eán* | if | Matt. 18:15 | 7 |
| *ebaptísthēmen* | were baptized | 1 Cor. 12:13 | 46 |
| *ebéblēto* | place oneself | Luke 16:20 | 35 |
| *échomai* | to hold | | 100 |
| *ēgapēménoi* | beloved ones | Col. 3:12 | 99 |
| *ēgápēsa* | have loved (aorist of *agapáō*) | John 15:9 | 42 |
| *egēgerménon* | to raise oneself | 2 Tim. 2:8 | 139 |
| *egḗgertai* | raised by himself | 1 Cor. 15:20 | 68 |
| *egéneto* | became | John 1:14 | 124 |
| *egkráteia* | temperance, self-control | Gal. 5:23 | 86 |
| *egṓ* | I | Rev. 1:8 | 165, 166 |
| *ei* | since, if (particle which usually denotes supposition) | Rom. 8:31; Col. 3:1 1 Pet. 1:7 | 7, 56 97, 160 |
| *eídos* | fashion, or external appearance of the face | | 28 |
| *eidótes* | knowing | Gal. 2:16 | 79 |

| | | | |
|---|---|---|---|
| *eilēphen,* see *lambánō* | | | |
| *eimí* | I am | Rev. 1:8 | 166 |
| *eirēnē* | peace | Gal. 5:22 | 86 |
| *eisenégkēs* | bring us into | Matt. 6:13 | 65 |
| *ek* (or *ex*) | out of | | 67, 78 |
| *ékbasis* | way of escape | 1 Cor. 10:13; Heb. 13:7 | 67 |
| *eklektoí* | chosen | Col. 3:12 | 99 |
| *ekpeirázōmen* | tempt | 1 Cor. 10:9 | 63 |
| *elégchō* | rebuke, reprove | | 8 |
| *élegxon,* see *elégchō* | | | |
| *elēlutha* | came | John 18:37 | 124 |
| *élthē* | is come | John 15:26 | 44 |
| *élthen,* see *élthē* | | 1 Tim. 1:15 | 126, 127 |
| *emáthete* | learned | Phil. 4:9 | 94 |
| *ēn* | was (imperfect of *eimí*) | Rev. 21:6 | 166 |
| *en* | in | 1 Cor. 12:13 | 46, 48, 60, 107, 121 |
| *en dólō* | in guile | | 107 |
| *endusámenoi* | put on | Col. 3:10 | 98 |
| *endúsasthe* | clothe | Col. 3:12 | 99 |
| *enedidúsketo* | to dress oneself | Luke 16:19 | 33 |

| | | | |
|---|---|---|---|
| *energḗs* | energizing, powerful | Heb. 4:12 | 18 |
| *épainos* | praise | Phil. 1:11 | 96 |
| *ephrouroúmetha* | keep under, keep guard | Gal. 3:24 | 81 |
| *epí* | upon | | 96 |
| *epieikḗs* | gentle, tolerant | Phil. 4:5; 1 Tim. 3:3; Titus 3:2; James 3:17 | 163 |
| *epígeios* | earthly | 2 Cor. 5:1 | 2 |
| *éprepe* | becoming, fitting | Heb. 2:10; 7:26 | 147 |
| *éprepen,* see *éprepe* | | | |
| *érchomai* | I come | Rev. 22:13 | 44, 124, 167 |
| *érōs* | love (selfish), lust | | 40, 41 |
| *estí* | is | John 14:28 | 125 |
| *eú* | well, good | | 34, 95, 101, 131, 132, 154 |
| *euaggélion* | good news, gospel | John 1:12; 3:16; 1 Tim. 4:10; 1 John 2:2 | 77 |
| *eucharistḗsas* | having given thanks | Luke 22:17; John 6:11, 23 | 102 |
| *eucharistía* | thanksgiving | 1 Thess. 1:2 | 101, 102 |
| *eudaímōn* | fortunate, happy because of favor shown | | 111 |
| *eulábeia* | caution, fear of God, circumspection | John 14:27; Heb. 5:7; 12:28 | 131, 137 |

| | | | |
|---|---|---|---|
| *eulogésas* | blessed | Matt. 26:26;<br>Mark 14:22 | 102 |
| *euperístatos*,<br>see *perístamai* | beset | Heb. 12:1 | 154 |
| *eúphēma* | good report | Phil. 4:8 | 95 |
| *euphraínō* | being merry,<br>happy | (for numerous<br>references, see text) | 111 |
| *euphrainómenos* | glad-minded,<br>feeling good and<br>having fun | Luke 16:19 | 34 |
| *eusébeia* | godliness | (for numerous<br>references, see text) | 131–134,<br>137, 138 |
| *eusebés* (adj.),<br>see *eusébeia* | | | |
| *eusebéō* (verb),<br>see *eusébeia* | | Acts 17:23;<br>1 Tim. 5:4 | |
| *eusebós* (adv.),<br>see *eusébeia* | | 2 Tim. 3:12;<br>Titus 2:12 | |
| *euthuméō* | being of good<br>cheer | Acts 27:22, 25;<br>James 5:13 | 111 |
| *euthúmōs* (adv.),<br>see *euthuméō* | | Acts 24:10 | 111 |
| *éuthumos* (adj.),<br>see *euthuméō* | | Acts 27:36 | 111 |
| *eutuchés* | one with good luck | | 111 |
| *exéletai* | might deliver | Gal. 1:4 | 77 |
| *exousía* | authority | | 30 |
| *gegénnēmai* | born | John 18:37 | 124 |
| *gégonen* | become | 2 Cor. 5:17 | 71 |

| | | | |
|---|---|---|---|
| *gennáō* | to give birth | | 124 |
| *gínesthe* | keep becoming | 1 Cor. 10:7 | 62 |
| *gínomai* | become | | 124 |
| *glṓssai* | languages, tongues | Acts 2:6, 8 | 48 |
| *gnṓnai*, see *gnṓsis* | | | |
| *gnṓsis* | experiential knowledge | Phil 3:9 | 91, 92 |
| *goggúzete* | murmur | 1 Cor. 10:10 | 63 |
| *hádēs* | hell | Luke 16:23 | 34, 35 |
| *hagiasmós* | sanctification | 2 Thess. 2:13 | 121 |
| *hagná* | pure, chaste | Phil. 4:8 | 95 |
| *hairéō* | to choose | | 120 |
| *hamártē* | sin (single) | 1 John 2:1 | 71 |
| *hamartḗsē* | trespass | Matt. 18:15 | 7 |
| *hḗ*, see *ho* | | | |
| *hēdonḗ* | hedonism, sensual pleasure | Luke 8:14; Titus 3:3; James 4:1, 3; 2 Pet. 2:13 | 110 |
| *heíleto*, see *hairéō* | | 2 Thess. 2:13 | 120 |
| *hḗpios* | gentle | 1 Thess. 1:7 | 108 |
| *hēlkōménos*, see *hélkos* | | | |
| *hélkos* | ulcer | Luke 16:21 | 35 |

| | | | |
|---|---|---|---|
| *hētérais* | qualitively different | John 14:15–17; 16:7–14 | 48 |
| *hetérō* | another of a different kind | Matt. 21:30; Gal. 1:6 | 11, 28, 78 100 |
| *heterodidaskalía* | teach otherwise | 1 Tim. 6:4 | 137 |
| *héteron,* see *hetérō* | | | |
| *héteros,* see *hetérō* | | | |
| *híēmi* | to send | | 115 |
| *ho* | the (definite article) | | 11, 31, 37–39, 59, 71, 81, 91, 122, 123, 149, 157, 166, 167 |
| *ho aiṓn ho erchómenos* | the next age | Mark 10:30; Luke 18:30 | 73 |
| *ho aiṓn hoútos* | this age | (for numerous references, see text) | 73 |
| *ho ṓn* | the one being | John 1:18 | 38 |
| *hōs* | according as | | 47 |
| *hósa* | as many as whatsoever | Phil. 4:8 | 94 |
| *huioí* | sons | Luke 15:11–32; Rom. 8:14 | 11, 54 |
| *hupér* | because of | Rom. 5:6–8 | 74 |
| *huperéchon* | excellency | Phil. 3:8 | 91 |
| *hupomonḗ* | patience | | 104 |
| *hústeron* | afterward | Matt. 21:29 | 11 |

| kagṓ | I myself (translated "so") | John 15:9 | 41 |
|---|---|---|---|
| kaí | and | Luke 10:9 | 31 |
| kainḗ | qualitatively new | 2 Cor. 5:17 | 70 |
| kainós | qualitively new | Rev. 21:1 | 167 |
| kakopáthēson | endure afflictions | 2 Tim. 4:5 | 140 |
| kakopathṓ | to suffer evils | 2 Tim. 2:9 | 140 |
| kapēleúō | to treat as if for personal profit | 2 Cor. 2:17 | 136 |
| karpós | fruit | Gal. 5:22; Eph. 5:9 | 85 |
| katá | according to, down (used as an intensive) | | 41, 156 |
| katallagḗ | reconciliation | Rom. 5:10; 2 Cor. 5:18–20 | 70 |
| katalúō | to put an end to a previous goal, to disunite, destroy (figuratively refers to loosening an application) | Matt. 26:61; 27:40; Mark 14:58; 15:29; Acts 6:14 | 156 |
| katērtisména | fitted | Rom. 9:22 | 121 |
| kathṓs | in the same manner as | John 15:9 | 41 |
| kaucháomai | boast | (for numerous references, see text on page given) | 112 |
| kékritai, see krínō | | | |
| kenḗ | vain, empty | 1 Thess. 2:1 | 106 |

| *kérdos* | profit, advantage | | 134 |
|---|---|---|---|
| *kópos* | fatigue resulting from labor | 1 Thess. 1:3 | 104 |
| *kosméo* | to beautify | | 72 |
| *kósmos* | world, universe | John 8:12 | 72, 73, 75 |
| *kósmou*<br>see *kósmos* | | | |
| *kríma* | present judgment | John 9:39 | 160 |
| *krínetai,*<br>see *kríno* | | | |
| *krínō* | to judge, separate, divide, distinguish, discern, select, or form an opinion | John 3:18; 1 Pet. 1:17; 3:9 | 159–161 |
| *krínonta,*<br>see *kríno* | | | |
| *krísis* | future judgment | | 160 |
| *kuriakḗ* | the first day of the Lord | Acts 20:7; 1 Cor. 16:2 | 16 |
| *kúrios* | Lord | Phil 3:8; Rev. 1:10 | 16, 92 |
| *laliá* | word | | 123 |
| *lambáno* | to take, to reach out and take hold of | | 66 |
| *lámpō* | to shine | | 34 |
| *lamprós* | shining, showing off | Luke 16:19 | 34 |
| *légō* | to speak intelligently | | 105 |

| | | | |
|---|---|---|---|
| *logízomai* | think, count | Phil. 3:13 | 93 |
| *lógos* | word, the Eternal Word (Jesus Christ) | John 1:14; 1 Tim. 1:15; 3:1; 4:9; 2 Tim. 2:11; Titus 3:8; Rev. 21:6 | 59, 122–124, 166, 167 |
| *lúō* | to loose, bind, perish | | 156 |
| *máchesthai* | to fight as if in war or battle | 2 Tim. 2:24 | 108 |
| *makárioi,* see *makários* | | | |
| *makários* | blessed | Matt. 5:3–12; Luke 6:20–23; John 15:11; James 1:12 | 1, 2, 65, 110, 111 |
| *makrothumía* | long-suffering | (for numerous references, see text on pages given) | 86, 100 |
| *marturía* | testimony | John 15:26 | 45 |
| *meínate* | continue | John 15:9 | 42 |
| *mēkúnetai* | lengthen | Mark 4:27 | 18 |
| *mélomai* | to care for oneself | Matt. 21:29 | 12 |
| *metá* | after | | 12, 28 |
| *metaméleia,* see *metá* and *mélomai* | a selfish change brought about by regret | Matt. 27:3 | 12 |
| *metamelētheís,* see *metá* and *mélomai* | | | 12, 13 |
| *metamelomai* see *metá* and *mélomai* | | | |

| | | | |
|---|---|---|---|
| *metemorphṓthē* | transfigured | Mark 9:2 | 28 |
| *metonoéō,* see *metánoia* | | | |
| *metánoēsas,* see *metánoia* | | | |
| *metánoia* | repentance | Matt. 3:2; 4:17 | 12 |
| *misthós* | pay for work done | | 138 |
| *mneía* | remembrance, mention | 1 Thess. 1:2 | 103 |
| *mnēmoneúontes* | to call to mind | Rom. 1:9; 2 Thess. 2:13 | 104 |
| *moicháō* | to commit adultery | Matt. 5:32; 19:19; Mark 10:11, 12 | 24 |
| *moichṓmai,* see *moicháō* | | | |
| *moichásthai,* see *moicháō* | | | |
| *moichátai,* see *moicháō* | | | |
| *moicheí,* see *moicheúō* | | | |
| *moicheúō* | commit adultery | Matt. 5:27, 28 19:18; Mark 10:19; Luke 16:18 | 24, 25 |
| *morphḗn* | form | Phil. 2:6–8 | 59 |
| *morphóō* | to form | | 28 |
| *muéō* | to initiate | | 59 |
| *múō* | to shut the eyes | | 59 |

| | | | |
|---|---|---|---|
| *mustḗria,* see *mustḗrion* | | | |
| *mustḗrion* | mystery | Rom. 16:25 | 59 |
| *noéō* | think, perceive | | 12 |
| *ógkos* | weight | Heb. 12:1 | 154 |
| *oída* | to know intuitively | | 79 |
| *oikétai* | household companions | 1 Pet. 2:18 | 162 |
| *oikṓ en* | dwell in | Rom. 7:17 | 53 |
| *ólethros* | destruction, ruin | 1 Cor. 5:5; 1 Thess. 5:3; 2 Thess. 1:9; 1 Tim. 6:9 | 156 |
| *olothreúō* | destroy, die | Heb. 11:28 | 156 |
| *ónkos,* see *ógkos* | | | |
| *opheílomen eucharisteín* | "we are bound to thank" | 2 Thess. 1:3 | 102 |
| *ou* | not | Matt. 21:29 | 11 |
| *oudeís* | no man, no created being | John 1:18 | 126 |
| *palaiá* | old | | 71 |
| *panḗguris* | general assembly (KJV) | Heb. 12:22 | 157 |
| *pánta,* see *pántes* | | | |
| *pántes* | all | 1 Cor. 3:1–3; 2 Cor. 5:17; Heb. 2:8 | 50, 71, 149 |

| | | | |
|---|---|---|---|
| *pántote* | always | 1 Thess. 1:2; 5:16 | 103, 110 |
| *paráklēsis* | exhortation, a calling near | 1 Thess. 2:3 | 107 |
| *paráklētos* | one who comes alongside | John 14:16, 26; 15:26; 16:7 | 43 |
| *paralambánō* | to accept | 1 Cor. 15:1, 3; Gal. 1:9; Phil. 4:9 | 94 |
| *parautíka* | transient | 2 Cor. 4:17 | 157 |
| *parédōken* | delivered up | Rom. 8:32 | 57 |
| *parelábete,* see *paralambánō* | | | |
| *parḗlthen* | gone forever, passed away | 2 Cor. 5:17 | 71 |
| *parrēsiázomai* | to speak boldy, bold in demeanor, speech, and action | 1 Thess. 2:2 | 106 |
| *parousía* | coming presence | 1 Thess. 4:15 | 116 |
| *peirasmós* | experience | Heb. 11:29, 36 | 64 |
| *peirázō* | to tempt | 1 Cor. 10:9 | 64 |
| *peírō* | to pierce through with a weapon(spear) | | 64 |
| *pémpō* | I send | John 20:21 | 30 |
| *perioúsios* | peculiar | Titus 2:14 | 2 |
| *peripatéō* | to walk about | | 84 |
| *periístamai* | to stand around | | 154 |
| *phéggos* | light | Matt. 24:29; Mark 13:24; Luke 21:25 | 114 |

| | | | |
|---|---|---|---|
| *phḗmē* | fame | | 95 |
| *phēmí* | speak, make known | | 95 |
| *philía* | love (friendship) | 2 Cor. 6:14; Phil. 4:8 | 40, 41, 95 |
| *philéō*, see *philía* | | | |
| *phílos* | friend | | 95 |
| *phōtisthéntes* | enlightened ones | Heb. 6:4; 10:32 | 84 |
| *phrḗn* | mind | | 34 |
| *phroneísthō* | "let this mind be in you" | Phil. 2:5 | 89 |
| *phroneíte* | "set your affection" | Col. 3:2 | 97 |
| *phrouréō* | to keep guard | | 81 |
| *piptóntōn* | kept falling | Luke 16:21 | 35 |
| *pístis* | faith | Gal. 3:18, 19; 5:22 | 81, 86 |
| *pisteúsasi* | believe (aorist participle) | Mark 16:17 | 31 |
| *pistós* | trustworthy, dependable, faithful | 1 Cor. 10:13 1 Tim. 1:15; 3:1; 4:9; 2 Tim. 2:11; Titus 3:8 | 67, 122, 123 |
| *pleonexía* | greediness | | 138 |
| *polloús* | proportionately | Heb. 2:10 | 150 |
| *ponērós* | malevolent, evil | John 17:5 | 76 |
| *porismós* | gain | 1 Tim. 6:5, 6 | 134, 138 |
| *póros* | the means of acquiring gain | | 134 |

| | | | |
|---|---|---|---|
| *pórnē* | harlot | 1 Cor. 6:15 | 23 |
| *praótēs* | meekness, active opposition to evil | Gal. 5:22; Col. 3:12 | 86, 100 |
| *prássete,* see *prássō* | | | |
| *prássō* | do | Phil. 4:9 | 94 |
| *prépei,* see *prépō* | | | |
| *prépō* | fitting, proper, right, consequently necessary | | 147 |
| *proētoímasen,* see *proetoimázō* | | | |
| *proetoimázō* | afore prepared | Rom. 9:23 | 121 |
| *próphasis* | cloak (figurative for a pretext, excuse) | 1 Thess 2:5 | 107 |
| *prophēteía* | prophecy, the telling forth | | 123 |
| *prós* | to | | 95 |
| *proseúxasthai,* see *proseúchomai* | | | |
| *proseúchomai* | to pray (habitually) | Luke 9:28 | 27 |
| *prosphilḗs* | lovely | Phil. 4:8 | 95 |
| *pseúdesthe,* see *pseúdomai* | | | |
| *pseúdomai* | to lie continually | Col. 3:9 | 98 |
| *ptōchós* | beggar | Luke 16:20 | 33 |
| *ptṓssō* | to crouch | | 33 |

| | | | |
|---|---|---|---|
| *rhḗma* | utterance | | 123 |
| *seb* (stem) | to fall back or forward | | 132 |
| *sébomai* | to reverence, venerate, worship | (for numerous references, see text on pages given) | 95, 131, 132 |
| *seíō* | shake | Heb. 12:26 | 158 |
| *semná,* see *semnós* | | | |
| *semnós* | honest | Phil. 4:8; 1 Tim. 3:8, 11; Tit. 2:2 | 95 |
| *sesigēménou,* see *sígaō* | | | |
| *sígaō* | to be silent | Rom. 16:25 | 61 |
| *skoliós* | crooked | Luke 3:5; Acts 2:40; Phil. 2:15 | 163 |
| *skotía* | darkness | Eph. 5:8 | 83 |
| *skótos,* see *skotía* | | | |
| *sōphronismós* | sound mind | 2 Tim. 1:7 | 89 |
| *sōtēría* | salvation | 2 Thess. 2:13 | 121 |
| *spéndomai* | offer, pour out | 2 Tim. 4:6 | 142 |
| *splágchna* | bowels (organs essential to the human body) | Col. 3:12 | 99 |
| *stenochōría* | distress | Rom. 8:35 | 58 |
| *stéphanos* | reward, crown | Matt. 27:29; Mark 15:17; John 19:2, 5; 2 Tim. 4:8; Rev. 1:6 | 141, 142 |

| | | | |
|---|---|---|---|
| *stēríxai,*<br>see *stērízō* | | | |
| *stērízō* | to make steadfast | Rom. 16:25 | 60 |
| *stoicheín,*<br>see *stoichéō* | | | |
| *stoichéō* | to walk | Acts 21:24; Rom.<br>4:12; Gal. 5:25;<br>6:16; Phil. 3:16 | 84, 85 |
| *stoichḗsousin,*<br>see *stoichéō* | | | |
| *stoichṓmen,*<br>see *stoichéō* | | | |
| *stoichós* | a row | | 84 |
| *summorphoúmenos* | made conformable | Phil. 3:8 | 92 |
| *sún* | together | | 167 |
| *suneídēsis* | conscience | 1 Pet. 2:19 | 164 |
| *sundoxasthṓmen* | to glorify together | Rom. 8:17 | 150 |
| *sunezōopoíēse* | quickened together | Eph. 2:5;<br>Col. 2:13 | 74 |
| *suntéleia toú<br>aiṓnos* | the consummation<br>of the age | Matt. 13:39, 40,<br>49; 24:3; Heb. 9:26;<br>Rev. 21:6 | 73, 167 |
| *tá,*<br>see *ho* | | | |
| *tachú* | quickly, soon | Rev. 22:12 | 167 |
| *tapeinophrosúnē* | humility | Col. 3:12 | 100 |
| *tássomai* | to place in the<br>proper category | | 5 |
| *taúta* | those things | Phil. 4:9 | 94 |

*tékna,*
see *téknon*

| *téknon* | children | Matt. 21:29; John 1:12; Rom. 8:16 | 11, 54, 55 |
|---|---|---|---|
| *teleióō* | to bring about a purpose, be made complete | Heb. 2:10; 11:40; 12:22; Rev. 21:6 | 148, 152, 158 |
| *téleios* | complete, perfect | Rev. 1:11 | 167 |

*teleiōsai,*
see *teleióō*

*teleiōthōsi,*
see *teleióō*

| *teléō* | to finish, complete | | 148 |
|---|---|---|---|
| *télos* | end | | 167 |

*teteleiōménōn,*
see *teleióō*

*tetélestai,*
see *teléō*

| *tetérēka* | keep | John 15:10 | 42 |
|---|---|---|---|
| *tetúphōtai* | to place a smoke-screen to deceive others | 1 Tim. 6:4 | 137 |

*thélei,*
see *thélō*

| *thélō* | to will, wish | Matt. 21:29; 1 Tim. 2:4 | 11, 130 |
|---|---|---|---|
| *theós* | God, the Father | John 3:16, 17; 1 Tim. 2:10 | 37, 39, 132 |
| *theosébeia,* | to reverence God | | 132 |

| | | | |
|---|---|---|---|
| *theosebḗs* | reverencing God godly | John 9:31 | 132 |
| *theostugḗs* | impious, hating God | Rom. 1:30 | 132 |
| *thliboménois* | afflicted, troubled | 2 Thess. 1:7 | 115 |
| *thlípsis* | circumstances, tribulation | Rom. 8:35 | 58, 115 |
| *tó,* see *ho* | | | |
| *tṓ,* see *ho* | | | |
| *toís,* see *ho* | | | |
| *tréchōmen* | to run | Heb. 12:1 | 153 |
| *zēteíte* | seek | Col. 3:1 | 97 |
| *zṓn* | living | Heb. 4:12 | 18 |
| *zōopoisḗsei* | quicken | Rom. 8:11 | 53 |
| *zóphos* | thick darkness, the gloom of the underworld | Heb. 12:18; 2 Pet. 2:4, 17; Jude 1:6, 13 | 83 |

# Scripture Index

## Genesis

| | |
|---|---|
| 1:4, 12, 18, 21, 25, 31 | 72 |
| 1:26 | 130 |
| 2:17 | 113, 162 |
| 2:24 | 22 |
| 3 | 72 |
| 3:16, 17 | 130 |
| 3:17 | 113 |
| 3:17–24 | 162 |

## Exodus

| | |
|---|---|
| 18:26 | 132 |
| 20:8 | 14 |
| 20:11 | 14 |
| 23:11 | 14 |
| 23:12 | 14 |
| 32:6 | 62 |

## Leviticus

| | |
|---|---|
| 20:10 | 22 |
| 23:16 | 44 |

## Numbers

| | |
|---|---|
| 14:22–30 | 63 |
| 21:4–6 | 63 |
| 25:1, 2 | 63 |

## Deuteronomy

| | |
|---|---|
| 5:14 | 14 |
| 5:15 | 14 |
| 22:21 | 22 |
| 24:1–4 | 22 |
| 24:4 | 23 |

## 2 Kings

| | |
|---|---|
| 2:1 | 28 |

## Job

| | |
|---|---|
| 1:1, 8 | 132 |
| 33:28, 30 | 84 |

## Psalms

| | |
|---|---|
| 4:6 | 84 |
| 27:1 | 84 |
| 36:9 | 84 |
| 43:3 | 84 |
| 56:13 | 84 |

## Proverbs

| | |
|---|---|
| 2:13 | 83 |
| 25:2 | 60 |

## Isaiah

| | |
|---|---|
| 2:12 | 116 |
| 5:20 | 83 |
| 10:17 | 84 |
| 13:6, 9 | 116 |
| 24:16 | 131 |
| 26:7 | 131 |
| 53:11 | 70 |
| 55:8, 9 | 120 |
| 60:2 | 83 |

## Ezekiel

| | |
|---|---|
| 13:5 | 116 |
| 30:3 | 116 |

## Daniel

| | |
|---|---|
| 7:7, 8, 19–27 | 114 |
| 9:24–27 | 114 |
| 11:36–45 | 114 |
| 12:1 | 114 |

## Joel

| | |
|---|---|
| 1:15 | 116 |
| 2:1, 11, 31 | 116 |
| 3:14 | 116 |

## Amos

| | |
|---|---|
| 5:18, 20 | 116 |

## Obadiah

| | |
|---|---|
| 1:15 | 116 |

## Micah

| | |
|---|---|
| 7:8 | 84 |
| 7:19 | 74 |

## Zephaniah

| | |
|---|---|
| 1:7, 14 | 116 |

## Zechariah

| | |
|---|---|
| 14:1 | 116 |

## Malachi

| | |
|---|---|
| 2:16 | 22 |
| 4:5 | 116 |

## Matthew

| | |
|---|---|
| 1:16, 20, 21 | 123 |
| 1:18, 20 | 37, 43 |
| 1:21 | 129 |
| 2:13 | 155 |
| 3:2 | 12, 17, 77 |
| 3:4–6 | 10 |
| 3:7–10 | 10 |
| 3:11 | 44, 46, 51, 70 |
| 4:1 | 64 |
| 4:3 | 20, 64 |
| 4:16 | 83 |
| 4:17 | 12 |
| 4:20 | 95 |
| 5:1–12 | 110 |
| 5:3–12 | 1 |
| 5:5 | 72 |
| 5:11 | 110 |
| 5:12 | 111 |
| 5:13 | 2 |
| 5:13, 14 | 1, 78 |
| 5:16 | 1, 2 |
| 5:17 | 16, 156 |
| 5:23, 24 | 144 |
| 5:27, 28 | 24 |
| 5:27–32 | 22 |
| 5:32 | 23, 24 |
| 5:44 | 40 |
| 6:19, 20 | 97 |
| 6:23 | 83 |
| 6:33 | 4, 156 |
| 7:1, 2 | 7 |
| 7:6 | 86 |
| 7:13 | 155 |
| 7:19, 20 | 85 |
| 7:21 | 98, 121 |
| 7:26 | 155 |
| 8:12 | 83 |
| 8:14, 15 | 15 |
| 8:25 | 155 |
| 10:5, 16, 40 | 30 |
| 10:28 | 155 |
| 11:23 | 35 |
| 11:28 | 129 |
| 12:3, 4 | 16 |
| 12:7 | 16 |
| 12:9–14 | 15 |
| 12:34 | 34 |
| 13:11 | 60 |
| 13:19ff | 85 |
| 13:22 | 72, 73 |
| 13:38 | 11 |
| 13:39, 40, 49 | 73, 167 |
| 15:3–20 | 16 |
| 15:9 | 131 |
| 16:1 | 64 |
| 16:16 | 26 |
| 16:21 | 19 |

| | | | |
|---|---|---|---|
| 16:21, 24 | 2 | 25:14–30 | 85 |
| 16:21–27 | 26 | 25:30 | 83 |
| 16:22, 23 | 20 | 25:31–46 | 73, 161 |
| 16:23 | 27 | 26:26 | 102 |
| 16:24 | 3, 5, 140 | 26:61 | 156 |
| 16:24–28 | 6 | 27:3 | 13 |
| 16:26 | 2, 4 | 27:20 | 155 |
| 16:28 | 27 | 27:29 | 141 |
| 17:1 | 26, 27 | 27:40 | 156 |
| 18:15 | 7, 8 | 27:46 | 125 |
| 18:16 | 9 | 27:51 | 158 |
| 18:17 | 9 | 27:57 | 33 |
| 19:2–12 | 22 | 28:4 | 158 |
| 19:9 | 24 | 28:20 | 167 |
| 19:16–22 | 4 | | |
| 19:18 | 24 | **Mark** | |
| 19:19 | 3 | 1:4 | 12 |
| 19:21 | 4 | 1:8 | 44, 46 |
| 19:23, 24 | 33 | 1:21–27 | 15 |
| 20:1–16 | 140 | 1:29–31 | 15 |
| 21:16 | 96 | 2:7 | 129 |
| 21:23 | 10 | 2:10 | 149 |
| 21:28 | 11 | 2:23–28 | 16 |
| 21:29 | 10–12 | 2:25, 26 | 16 |
| 21:29, 32 | 13 | 2:27 | 14 |
| 21:31, 32 | 10 | 3:1–6 | 15 |
| 21:33–46 | 85 | 4:11 | 60 |
| 21:45, 46 | 10 | 4:15ff | 85 |
| 22:7 | 155 | 4:26 | 17 |
| 22:13 | 83 | 4:26–29 | 17 |
| 22:18, 35 | 64 | 4:27 | 17 |
| 22:39 | 3 | 4:28 | 18 |
| 23:13–33 | 16 | 4:29 | 18 |
| 24:3 | 73, 167 | 7:7 | 131 |
| 24:15 | 114 | 8:29 | 26 |
| 24:21 | 113, 114 | 8:31 | 19, 21 |
| 24:21, 29 | 113 | 8:31–37 | 26 |
| 24:29 | 114 | 8:33 | 27 |
| 24:29–30 | 114 | 8:34 | 5, 20 |
| 24:29–31 | 158 | 8:35 | 19 |
| 24:36 | 126 | 8:34—9:1 | 6 |
| 24:44 | 27 | 8:36 | 2, 136 |
| 24:45–51 | 140 | 9:1 | 27 |

| | |
|---|---|
| 9:2 | 26, 27 |
| 10:2–12 | 22 |
| 10:5 | 22 |
| 10:9 | 22 |
| 10:11, 12 | 25 |
| 10:17–22 | 4 |
| 10:19 | 24 |
| 10:30 | 73 |
| 12:1–12 | 85 |
| 12:31 | 3 |
| 13:14 | 114 |
| 13:19 | 114 |
| 13:19, 24 | 113 |
| 13:24 | 114 |
| 13:24–26 | 114 |
| 13:32 | 126 |
| 13:32, 33 | 27 |
| 14:4 | 155 |
| 14:22 | 102 |
| 14:58 | 156 |
| 15:17 | 141 |
| 15:29 | 156 |
| 16:5 | 28 |
| 16:15 | 121 |
| 16:17 | 31, 49 |

## Luke

| | |
|---|---|
| 1:14, 44 | 111 |
| 1:15 | 43 |
| 1:26–35 | 123 |
| 1:35 | 38 |
| 1:41, 67 | 43 |
| 1:47 | 111, 129 |
| 1:79 | 83 |
| 2:25 | 43 |
| 2:36 | 43 |
| 3:3 | 12 |
| 3:5 | 163 |
| 3:16 | 44, 46 |
| 4:18 | 43, 163 |
| 4:33–37 | 15 |
| 4:38, 39 | 15 |
| 5:37 | 155 |

| | |
|---|---|
| 6:6–11 | 15 |
| 6:20–23 | 110 |
| 6:22 | 110 |
| 6:27, 35 | 40 |
| 7:22 | 163 |
| 7:42, 43 | 100 |
| 8:3 | 33 |
| 8:10 | 60 |
| 8:11 | 17 |
| 8:12ff | 85 |
| 8:14 | 110 |
| 9:20 | 26 |
| 9:21–26 | 26 |
| 9:22 | 19 |
| 9:23 | 5 |
| 9:23–27 | 6 |
| 9:25 | 2 |
| 9:27 | 27 |
| 9:28 | 26, 27 |
| 9:29 | 26 |
| 9:48 | 30 |
| 10:1 | 29, 30 |
| 10:2 | 29 |
| 10:9 | 31 |
| 10:15 | 35 |
| 10:16 | 30 |
| 10:17 | 31 |
| 10:20 | 29 |
| 10:21 | 111 |
| 10:27 | 3 |
| 11:35 | 83 |
| 12:15 | 146 |
| 12:19 | 111 |
| 12:36–48 | 140 |
| 12:40, 46 | 27 |
| 13:5 | 155 |
| 13:10–17 | 15 |
| 14:1–6 | 15 |
| 14:26 | 3 |
| 14:33 | 3, 5 |
| 15:4, 6 | 155 |
| 15:11–32 | 11 |
| 15:23, 24, 29, 32 | 111 |

| | | | |
|---|---|---|---|
| 15:24 | 155 | 3:18 | 160 |
| 16:8 | 72, 73 | 3:18, 36 | 35 |
| 16:13 | 162 | 3:19 | 83 |
| 16:18 | 22, 24, 25 | 3:20 | 87 |
| 16:19 | 34, 111 | 5:5–18 | 15 |
| 16:20 | 33 | 5:24 | 70 |
| 16:22–24 | 156 | 5:25 | 69 |
| 16:25 | 33 | 5:35 | 111 |
| 17:20, 21 | 17 | 6:6 | 64 |
| 18:18–23 | 4 | 6:11, 23 | 102 |
| 18:23, 25 | 33 | 6:27 | 155 |
| 18:30 | 73 | 6:37 | 129, 130 |
| 18:43 | 96 | 8:12 | 2, 83 |
| 19:2 | 33 | 8:39, 56 | 35 |
| 19:11–27 | 85 | 8:56 | 111 |
| 20:9–19 | 85 | 9:1–16 | 15 |
| 20:34 | 72, 73 | 9:31 | 132 |
| 21:20 | 114 | 9:39 | 160 |
| 21:25 | 114 | 10:9 | 70 |
| 21:25–27 | 114 | 10:10 | 124 |
| 22:53 | 83 | 10:15 | 125 |
| 22:17 | 102 | 10:18 | 19 |
| | | 10:26–30 | 130 |

### John

| | | | |
|---|---|---|---|
| | | 10:28 | 155 |
| 1:1 | 43, 121, 123, 166 | 10:28–29 | 57, 60 |
| 1:1, 14 | 59, 122 | 10:30 | 90, 125 |
| 1:3, 4 | 91 | 10:38 | 125 |
| 1:5 | 83 | 11:25 | 69, 70, 156 |
| 1:12 | 54, 55, 77 | 12:16, 23, 28 | 150 |
| 1:14 | 19, 43, 60, 123 | 12:24 | 85, 156 |
| 1:18 | 38, 126 | 12:35, 46 | 83 |
| 1:29, 36 | 73 | 12:46 | 124 |
| 1:33 | 44, 46 | 13:17 | 111 |
| 3:2 | 37 | 13:31, 32 | 150 |
| 3:3 | 37, 54 | 14:6 | 70 |
| 3:5 | 38 | 14:11 | 125 |
| 3:9 | 39 | 14:13 | 150 |
| 3:12 | 37 | 14:15–17 | 48 |
| 3:13 | 39 | 14:16 | 49 |
| 3:16 | 5, 37, 39, 77, | 14:16, 26 | 43 |
| | 92, 129, 130, 155 | 14:17 | 49, 50 |
| 3:17 | 38, 129 | 14:20 | 125 |
| | | 14:27 | 137 |

| | | | |
|---|---|---|---|
| 14:28 | 125 | 2:4, 6, 8, 11 | 45 |
| 15:5 | 85 | 2:6, 8 | 48 |
| 15:8 | 150 | 2:20 | 116 |
| 15:9 | 41, 42 | 2:26 | 111 |
| 15:10 | 40 | 2:27, 31 | 35 |
| 15:11 | 109, 110 | 2:38 | 12, 77 |
| 15:16 | 130 | 2:40 | 163 |
| 15:18–25 | 78 | 2:46 | 109, 111, 112 |
| 15:20 | 113, 140 | 3:12 | 131 |
| 15:26 | 43–45 | 3:13, 25 | 35 |
| 16:7, 8 | 43 | 3:15 | 148 |
| 16:7–14 | 48 | 4:12 | 80 |
| 16:8 | 50 | 5:38, 39 | 156 |
| 16:13 | 52 | 6:14 | 156 |
| 16:13, 14 | 43, 45 | 7:41 | 111 |
| 16:16, 17 | 49 | 8:9–25 | 46 |
| 16:16–20 | 49 | 8:12 | 51 |
| 16:20 | 109 | 8:13 | 52 |
| 16:28 | 124 | 8:14 | 51 |
| 16:33 | 36, 113, 153 | 8:15 | 51 |
| 17:3 | 146 | 8:15, 17 | 51 |
| 17:6, 9, 12–20 | 73 | 8:17 | 51 |
| 17:6–16 | 78 | 8:18, 19 | 51 |
| 17:9–18 | 75 | 8:21 | 52 |
| 17:12 | 13, 155 | 8:22, 23 | 52 |
| 17:14 | 78 | 8:32 | 73 |
| 17:15 | 75 | 8:39 | 109, 112 |
| 17:21 | 100 | 9:5 | 130 |
| 17:23, 26 | 70 | 9:16 | 140 |
| 18:37 | 124 | 9:27, 29 | 106 |
| 19:2, 5 | 141 | 10:2, 7 | 131 |
| 19:38–42 | 39 | 10:7 | 162 |
| 20:21 | 30 | 10:30 | 133 |
| | | 10:34 | 79 |
| **Acts** | | 10:42 | 73, 161 |
| | | 10:43–48 | 133 |
| 1:5 | 47, 49 | 10:44–48 | 44, 51 |
| 1:8 | 44 | 10:46 | 45 |
| 1:10 | 28 | 11:15, 16 | 48 |
| 1:10, 11 | 44 | 11:15–18 | 44 |
| 2:1–13 | 47 | 11:18 | 133 |
| 2:1–42 | 44 | 13:15 | 107 |
| 2:4 | 46 | 13:26 | 35 |

| | |
|---|---|
| 13:43, 50 | 131 |
| 13:46 | 106 |
| 13:52 | 109, 112 |
| 14:3 | 106 |
| 14:17 | 111 |
| 14:22 | 113 |
| 15:31 | 107 |
| 16:14 | 33, 131 |
| 16:30, 31 | 80 |
| 16:34 | 109, 111, 112 |
| 17:1, 2 | 105 |
| 17:1–9 | 105 |
| 17:2 | 105 |
| 17:3 | 105 |
| 17:4 | 106 |
| 17:4, 17 | 130 |
| 17:5 | 105, 106 |
| 17:17 | 105 |
| 17:23 | 132 |
| 17:31 | 73, 161 |
| 18:4 | 105 |
| 18:7, 13 | 131 |
| 18:19 | 104 |
| 18:26 | 106 |
| 19:1–7 | 47, 49 |
| 19:1–17 | 44 |
| 19:4 | 127 |
| 19:6 | 45 |
| 19:8 | 104, 105 |
| 19:27 | 131 |
| 20:7 | 16 |
| 20:7, 9 | 105 |
| 20:24 | 112 |
| 21:24 | 84 |
| 22:12 | 131 |
| 24:10 | 111 |
| 24:25 | 73, 74, 105 |
| 26:2 | 111 |
| 26:18 | 83, 84 |
| 27:22, 25 | 111 |
| 27:36 | 111 |

## Romans

| | |
|---|---|
| 1:9 | 103, 104 |
| 1:16 | 19 |
| 1:18 | 131 |
| 1:21 | 102 |
| 1:24 | 107 |
| 1:30 | 131 |
| 2:1–3, 17 | 79 |
| 2:4 | 99, 100 |
| 2:5 | 23, 119 |
| 2:11 | 79 |
| 2:12 | 155 |
| 2:17, 23 | 112 |
| 2:19 | 83 |
| 3:12 | 100 |
| 3:23 | 77, 130, 147 |
| 3:24 | 127 |
| 3:24, 26, 28 | 132 |
| 4:3, 9, 12, 16 | 35 |
| 4:5 | 131 |
| 4:6 | 57 |
| 4:12 | 84 |
| 5:1 | 74, 78, 133, 151 |
| 5:1, 9 | 132 |
| 5:2, 3, 11 | 112 |
| 5:3 | 113 |
| 5:6 | 131 |
| 5:6, 8 | 148 |
| 5:6–8 | 74 |
| 5:9 | 80 |
| 5:10 | 70 |
| 5:11 | 112 |
| 5:12 | 151 |
| 5:12–21 | 127 |
| 5:20 | 62 |
| 6:3–6 | 97 |
| 6:4 | 84 |
| 6:6 | 71 |
| 6:9 | 156 |
| 6:19 | 107 |
| 6:21 | 87 |
| 6:23 | 127 |

| | | | |
|---|---|---|---|
| 7:1–3 | 22 | 11:22 | 100 |
| 7:5 | 87 | 11:26 | 130 |
| 7:7–12 | 79 | 12:2 | 98 |
| 7:17 | 4, 53 | 12:12 | 109, 113 |
| 7:22, 23 | 53 | 13:1–7 | 129 |
| 8:1 | 70, 82 | 13:12 | 83 |
| 8:2 | 2 | 14:4 | 162 |
| 8:2, 4 | 82 | 14:17 | 109, 112 |
| 8:7, 8 | 70 | 14:19 | 153 |
| 8:9 | 53 | 14:20 | 156 |
| 8:9–11 | 53 | 14:22 | 111 |
| 8:10 | 70 | 15:3 | 112 |
| 8:11 | 53 | 15:10 | 111 |
| 8:11, 14 | 53 | 15:13 | 109, 112 |
| 8:12 | 54 | 16:18 | 137 |
| 8:13 | 54 | 16:19 | 112 |
| 8:13, 14 | 54 | 16:25 | 59–61 |
| 8:14 | 50, 53–55 | 16:26, 27 | 61 |
| 8:16 | 54 | | |
| 8:17 | 150 | | |
| 8:18–25 | 158 | | |

## 1 Corinthians

| | | | |
|---|---|---|---|
| 8:19–23 | 66, 73 | 1:3 | 153 |
| 8:21 | 50 | 1:4 | 103 |
| 8:23 | 73 | 1:20 | 72, 73 |
| 8:28 | 67 | 1:23 | 147 |
| 8:29 | 120, 130 | 1:29, 31 | 112 |
| 8:30 | 120 | 1:30 | 57, 70 |
| 8:31 | 56 | 2:6 | 73 |
| 8:31–38 | 56 | 2:7 | 60 |
| 8:32 | 57 | 2:14 | 60 |
| 8:33 | 58 | 3:1–3 | 50 |
| 8:35 | 58, 113 | 3:6, 7 | 17 |
| 8:37 | 113 | 3:11–15 | 87 |
| 8:38, 39 | 58, 70 | 3:13–15 | 119 |
| 9:1–10, 18 | 13 | 3:16 | 43 |
| 9:22 | 100, 121, 155 | 3:21 | 112 |
| 9:23 | 120 | 4:5 | 83 |
| 10:8–11 | 70 | 4:7 | 112 |
| 10:9 | 80 | 5:5 | 117, 143, 156 |
| 10:9, 10 | 77 | 5:8 | 94 |
| 10:17 | 78 | 5:9, 10 | 73 |
| 10:18–21 | 13 | 6:2 | 150 |
| 11 | 13 | 6:9, 10 | 1 |

| | | | |
|---|---|---|---|
| 6:11 | 2 | 1:24 | 109, 110, 112 |
| 6:15 | 23 | 2:2 | 111 |
| 6:19 | 23 | 2:7, 10 | 100 |
| 7 | 22 | 2:17 | 136 |
| 7:15 | 153 | 4:17, 18 | 156 |
| 7:40 | 111 | 4:18 | 157 |
| 9:11, 12 | 108 | 5:1 | 2 |
| 10:7 | 62 | 5:7 | 84 |
| 10:7–10 | 62 | 5:10 | 119, 143, 161 |
| 10:8 | 62 | 5:12 | 112 |
| 10:9 | 63, 64 | 5:17 | 70, 75, 110, 128 |
| 10:10 | 63 | 5:18–20 | 70 |
| 10:11 | 62, 63 | 5:21 | 75, 127 |
| 10:13 | 64, 65, 67 | 6:6 | 100 |
| 12:10, 28, 30 | 49 | 6:10 | 2, 112 |
| 12:13 | 45, 46, 48, | 6:14 | 40, 83 |
| | 49, 52 | 7:4 | 86, 112, 113 |
| 12:14–27 | 46 | 7:14 | 112 |
| 13:1, 8 | 49 | 8:2 | 109 |
| 13:6 | 112 | 9:2 | 112 |
| 13:9 | 59 | 9:8 | 138 |
| 13:12 | 59 | 9:10 | 57 |
| 14:2, 4, 13, 19, 26, 27 | 48 | 10:8, 13, 15, 17 | 112 |
| 14:5, 6, 18, 22 | 49 | 11:2 | 95 |
| 15:1, 3 | 94 | 11:12, 16, 18, 30 | 112 |
| 15:3 | 78, 148 | 11:19–33 | 113 |
| 15:4 | 78 | 11:22–33 | 101 |
| 15:4–11 | 68 | 12:1, 5, 6, 9 | 112 |
| 15:10 | 109 | 12:13 | 100 |
| 15:12–18 | 68 | 12:21 | 107 |
| 15:19 | 68 | 13:5 | 64 |
| 15:20 | 68, 69 | 13:11 | 109 |
| 15:20–22, 51–55 | 73 | | |
| 15:22, 23 | 139 | **Galatians** | |
| 15:51, 52 | 28 | 1:3, 6 | 77 |
| 15:52 | 168 | 1:4 | 72, 73, 75, 77 |
| 16:2 | 16 | 1:5 | 75 |
| | | 1:6 | 78 |
| **2 Corinthians** | | 1:8 | 77 |
| 1:4 | 113 | 1:9 | 94 |
| 1:8–11 | 101 | 2:15 | 79 |
| 1:14 | 112, 117, 143 | 2:16 | 74, 78, 79 |
| 1:21, 22 | 51 | 2:17, 18 | 80 |

| | | | |
|---|---|---|---|
| 2:20 | 70, 80, 97 | 5:9 | 57, 85 |
| 3:6–9, 16, 18, 29 | 35 | 5:10 | 86 |
| 3:8, 9 | 81 | 5:11 | 86 |
| 3:13 | 82 | 5:13 | 84 |
| 3:19 | 81 | 5:20 | 103 |
| 3:24 | 81 | 5:32 | 60 |
| 4:4 | 38 | 6:9 | 79 |
| 4:6 | 43 | 6:12 | 83 |
| 4:27 | 111 | 6:19 | 60 |
| 5:1 | 82 | 6:20 | 106 |
| 5:16 | 82 | 6:23 | 153 |
| 5:19 | 107 | | |
| 5:19–21 | 54, 87 | | |

## Philippians

| | | | |
|---|---|---|---|
| 5:22 | 100, 109 | 1:4, 5 | 112 |
| 5:22, 23 | 85, 86, 133 | 1:6, 10 | 117, 143 |
| 5:25 | 84 | 1:11 | 96 |
| 6:13, 14 | 112 | 1:18 | 94 |
| 6:16 | 84, 85 | 1:20 | 68 |
| | | 1:21 | 21, 94, 134, 156 |

## Ephesians

| | | | |
|---|---|---|---|
| | | 1:21, 23 | 150 |
| 1:13 | 53 | 1:23 | 68 |
| 1:13, 14 | 51 | 1:25 | 109, 110, 112 |
| 1:16 | 103 | 1:28 | 155 |
| 2:1 | 74 | 2:2, 17 | 112 |
| 2:2 | 72, 73 | 2:3 | 91 |
| 2:5 | 74 | 2:5 | 89 |
| 2:7 | 100 | 2:6, 7 | 90 |
| 2:8 | 4, 70 | 2:6–8 | 59, 68, 126, |
| 2:8, 9 | 78, 133 | | 149, 168 |
| 2:8–10 | 168 | 2:8, 9 | 90 |
| 2:9 | 112 | 2:15 | 163 |
| 2:10 | 55, 57 | 2:16 | 117, 143 |
| 3:4 | 60 | 3:1 | 109 |
| 3:13 | 113 | 3:3 | 112 |
| 4:5 | 45 | 3:7 | 134 |
| 4:16 | 18 | 3:8 | 91, 112 |
| 4:19 | 107 | 3:9 | 91 |
| 4:30 | 53 | 3:10 | 92 |
| 4:31 | 144 | 3:11 | 92 |
| 5:1 | 88 | 3:12 | 84, 91 |
| 5:3 | 107 | 3:13 | 93 |
| 5:8 | 83 | 3:16 | 84, 85 |
| 5:8, 11 | 83 | 3:18 | 137 |

| | |
|---|---|
| 3:19 | 155 |
| 4:1 | 112 |
| 4:1–10 | 112 |
| 4:4 | 109 |
| 4:5 | 163 |
| 4:8 | 93–96 |
| 4:9 | 94, 96 |
| 4:20 | 75 |

## Colossians

| | |
|---|---|
| 1:3 | 103 |
| 1:11 | 109 |
| 1:11, 24 | 86 |
| 1:13 | 83 |
| 1:17 | 91, 149 |
| 1:18 | 150 |
| 1:24 | 109, 112 |
| 1:27 | 70, 110 |
| 2:2 | 30 |
| 2:9 | 122 |
| 2:12 | 97 |
| 2:13 | 74 |
| 3:1 | 97 |
| 3:2 | 97 |
| 3:5 | 98, 107 |
| 3:5–9 | 87 |
| 3:6, 7 | 98 |
| 3:8 | 98 |
| 3:9 | 3, 98 |
| 3:12 | 99 |
| 3:13 | 100 |
| 3:25 | 79 |
| 4:2 | 103 |
| 4:3 | 60 |
| 4:9 | 144 |
| 4:12 | 103 |

## 1 Thessalonians

| | |
|---|---|
| 1—2 | 102 |
| 1:2 | 101–104 |
| 1:3 | 104 |
| 1:6 | 86, 109 |
| 2:1 | 106 |

| | |
|---|---|
| 2:2 | 106 |
| 2:3 | 107 |
| 2:4 | 105, 107 |
| 2:5 | 107 |
| 2:6 | 108 |
| 2:7 | 108 |
| 2:10 | 106 |
| 2:19 | 112 |
| 3:5 | 64 |
| 3:5, 6 | 106 |
| 3:6 | 103 |
| 3:8 | 108 |
| 3:9 | 109, 112 |
| 3:13 | 60, 150 |
| 4:7 | 107 |
| 4:13–17 | 69 |
| 4:13–18 | 116 |
| 4:14 | 156 |
| 4:14–17 | 73 |
| 4:15 | 116 |
| 4:16 | 28, 116 |
| 4:17 | 28 |
| 5:2 | 116 |
| 5:3 | 156 |
| 5:4, 5 | 83 |
| 5:5 | 84 |
| 5:16 | 109, 110 |
| 5:18 | 101 |

## 2 Thessalonians

| | |
|---|---|
| 1:3 | 102–104 |
| 1:3, 11 | 103 |
| 1:4 | 113, 114, 118 |
| 1:5 | 115, 118 |
| 1:5, 11 | 119 |
| 1:6 | 115, 119 |
| 1:7 | 113, 116, 119 |
| 1:8 | 116, 118, 119 |
| 1:9 | 117, 156 |
| 1:10 | 117 |
| 2:2 | 143 |
| 2:3 | 155 |
| 2:13 | 102–104, 120, 121 |

| | |
|---|---|
| 2:14 | 121 |
| 2:15 | 121 |
| 2:17 | 60 |
| 3:3 | 30 |
| 3:7–9 | 108 |

## 1 Timothy
| | |
|---|---|
| 1:9 | 131 |
| 1:15 | 122, 126–129 |
| 1:16 | 100 |
| 1:17 | 75 |
| 2:1 | 129 |
| 2:2 | 129, 131, 134 |
| 2:3, 5 | 129 |
| 2:4 | 129, 130 |
| 2:4, 6 | 129 |
| 2:10 | 132 |
| 3:1 | 122 |
| 3:2 | 107 |
| 3:3 | 163 |
| 3:8 | 95, 138 |
| 3:11 | 95 |
| 3:16 | 131, 134 |
| 4:7, 8 | 131, 134 |
| 4:9 | 122, 128 |
| 4:10 | 77 |
| 5:4 | 132 |
| 5:18 | 138 |
| 5:22 | 95 |
| 6:3 | 137 |
| 6:3, 5, 6, 11 | 131, 134 |
| 6:4 | 137 |
| 6:5 | 135, 137, 138 |
| 6:5, 6 | 134 |
| 6:6 | 131, 134, 135, 137, 138 |
| 6:9 | 155, 156 |
| 6:17 | 72, 73 |

## 2 Timothy
| | |
|---|---|
| 1:7 | 89 |
| 1:12, 18 | 143 |
| 2:8 | 139 |
| 2:9 | 140 |
| 2:9, 10 | 139 |
| 2:11 | 122, 139, 140 |
| 2:16 | 130 |
| 2:24 | 108 |
| 3:5 | 131, 134 |
| 3:12 | 131 |
| 3:12, 13 | 118 |
| 4:1 | 161 |
| 4:5 | 140 |
| 4:6 | 142 |
| 4:7 | 142 |
| 4:8 | 119, 141, 143 |
| 4:10 | 72, 73 |
| 4:18 | 75 |

## Titus
| | |
|---|---|
| 1:1 | 131, 134 |
| 1:6 | 107 |
| 1:7 | 138 |
| 1:11 | 134 |
| 2:2 | 95 |
| 2:5 | 95 |
| 2:12 | 72, 73, 131, 132 |
| 2:14 | 2 |
| 3:2 | 163 |
| 3:3 | 110 |
| 3:4 | 100 |
| 3:5 | 57 |
| 3:8 | 122 |

## Philemon
| | |
|---|---|
| 1:2, 19 | 144 |
| 1:4 | 103 |
| 1:10 | 144 |
| 1:11, 12 | 144 |
| 1:12 | 144 |
| 1:14–16 | 145 |

## Hebrews
| | |
|---|---|
| 1:9 | 111 |
| 2:6–8 | 113 |

| | | | |
|---|---|---|---|
| 2:7 | 148 | 1:22 | 78 |
| 2:8 | 149 | 2:1 | 79 |
| 2:9 | 146, 147 | 2:5 | 163 |
| 2:10 | 146, 147, 150 | 2:14, 17, 18 | 78 |
| 2:17 | 146 | 2:17 | 133 |
| 4:12 | 18 | 2:21, 23 | 35 |
| 4:15 | 38, 147 | 3:17 | 86, 163 |
| 5:7 | 131 | 4:1, 3 | 110 |
| 5:9 | 148 | 4:7 | 65 |
| 6:4 | 84 | 4:16 | 112 |
| 7:26 | 147 | 5:6 | 79 |
| 9:12, 14 | 146 | 5:11 | 111 |
| 9:22 | 19, 126 | 5:13 | 111 |

## 1 Peter

| | | | |
|---|---|---|---|
| 9:26 | 73, 167 | | |
| 9:27 | 156 | 1:5 | 73 |
| 10:10 | 71 | 1:6, 8 | 111, 112 |
| 10:30 | 118 | 1:7 | 155 |
| 10:32 | 84 | 1:8 | 109, 112 |
| 10:34 | 112 | 1:17 | 159–161 |
| 10:39 | 155 | 1:19 | 73 |
| 11:8 | 35 | 2:9 | 83, 84 |
| 11:17 | 64 | 2:18 | 162 |
| 11:28 | 156 | 2:18, 19 | 162 |
| 11:29, 36 | 64 | 2:19 | 163 |
| 12:1 | 150, 151 | 2:22 | 107 |
| 12:2 | 148 | 3:2 | 95 |
| 12:15 | 144 | 3:14 | 111 |
| 12:18 | 83 | 3:18 | 147 |
| 12:22 | 157 | 3:20 | 100 |
| 12:26 | 155, 158 | 4:11 | 75 |
| 12:28 | 131 | 4:13 | 86, 109, 112 |
| 13:7 | 67 | 4:14 | 111 |
| 13:21 | 75 | 4:18 | 131 |
| | | 5:2 | 138 |

## James

| | | | |
|---|---|---|---|
| | | 5:10 | 60 |
| 1:2 | 86, 109 | 5:11 | 75 |
| 1:8 | 89 | | |
| 1:9 | 112 | | |
| 1:12 | 65 | ## 2 Peter | |
| 1:12–15 | 65 | 1:3–5 | 95 |
| 1:13 | 66 | 1:3, 6, 7 | 131 |
| 1:13, 14 | 64 | 1:4 | 1, 20, 38 |
| 1:14 | 66 | 2:1 | 155 |

| | |
|---|---|
| 2:4, 17 | 83 |
| 2:5 | 131 |
| 2:6 | 131 |
| 2:9 | 131 |
| 2:13 | 110 |
| 2:17 | 83 |
| 3:7 | 131, 155 |
| 3:9 | 130, 159 |
| 3:10 | 116 |
| 3:11 | 131 |
| 3:13 | 150 |
| 3:15 | 100 |
| 3:16 | 155 |

## 1 John

| | |
|---|---|
| 1:5 | 84 |
| 1:5, 6 | 83 |
| 1:8 | 99 |
| 1:9 | 23, 77 |
| 2:1 | 71 |
| 2:2 | 77 |
| 2:8 | 84 |
| 2:8, 9, 11 | 83 |
| 2:15 | 78 |
| 2:22 | 78 |
| 3:2 | 59, 158 |
| 3:3 | 95 |
| 3:6 | 54, 71 |
| 3:7, 10 | 57 |
| 3:10, 14, 23 | 78 |
| 3:13 | 78 |
| 4:7, 8, 11, 12, 19–21 | 78 |
| 5:2 | 78 |

## Jude

| | |
|---|---|
| 1:4, 15 | 131 |
| 1:6, 13 | 83 |
| 1:15 | 131 |
| 1:15, 18 | 131 |
| 1:24 | 111, 112 |

## Revelation

| | |
|---|---|
| 1:5 | 150 |
| 1:6 | 142 |
| 1:8 | 165 |
| 1:9 | 113 |
| 1:10 | 16 |
| 1:18 | 75, 139 |
| 2:6 | 168 |
| 2:9, 10 | 113 |
| 3:4 | 28 |
| 3:14 | 166 |
| 3:17 | 2 |
| 4—19 | 114, 115 |
| 4:9, 10 | 75 |
| 5:13, 14 | 75 |
| 7:12 | 75 |
| 10:6 | 75 |
| 11:10 | 111 |
| 11:15 | 75 |
| 12:12 | 111 |
| 13:8 | 32 |
| 14:11 | 75 |
| 15:3 | 23 |
| 15:7 | 75 |
| 16:5, 7 | 23 |
| 17:8 | 32 |
| 17:8, 11 | 155 |
| 18:12 | 33, 34 |
| 19:2 | 23 |
| 19:3 | 75 |
| 19:7 | 112 |
| 20:10 | 75 |
| 20:11–15 | 73, 115 |
| 20:12 | 32 |
| 21 | 158 |
| 21:1 | 73, 150, 167 |
| 21:6 | 165, 166 |
| 21:27 | 32 |
| 22:5 | 75 |
| 22:12 | 167 |
| 22:13 | 165, 167 |